VICTORIA AND

CHIHULY a

t the V&A

Edited by Jennifer Hawkins Opie
V&A Publications in association with Portland Press

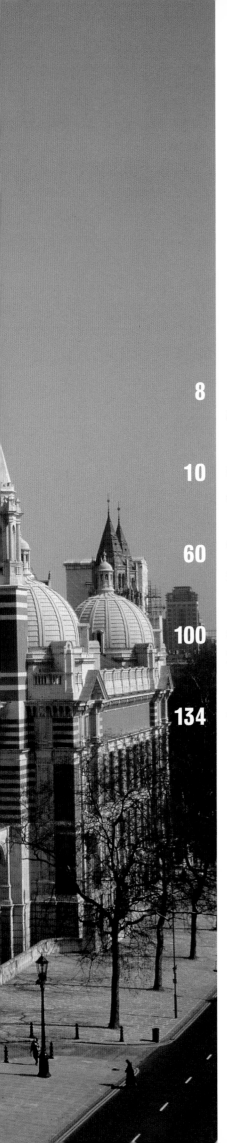

JPMorgan

JPMorgan, the investment bank of J.P. Morgan Chase & Co., is delighted to support this landmark exhibition of Dale Chihuly's work at the Victoria and Albert Museum in London, the first full-scale exhibition of his work in the UK. These exciting innovations, each informed by the best traditions of the past, find a perfect setting at the V&A, home to one of the world's greatest collections of Venetian glass. Chihuly's European roots and extensive study of the living tradition of Venetian glassmaking inspire Chihuly's American aesthetic, contemporary yet reflective.

The JPMorgan Chase Art Collection has included Chihuly pieces since 1983. This sponsorship, one of the first undertaken by our merged firm, combines the long Morgan tradition of support for the arts with Chase's renowned commitment to contemporary art. We are proud to sponsor this spectacular exhibition, bringing together the new world and the old, the past and the present—and encompassing our vision for the future.

Late one night in October 1999, I stood on the walls of Jerusalem and marvelled at an extraordinary creation: it was another wall, made not of stone but of clear Alaskan ice, cut into large rectangular blocks and carefully assembled to make an alternative wall for the city. The effect was magical, with light, both clear and coloured, animating the structure and revealing the complex patterns and striations that lay within the frozen blocks. By day, in the warm sun, the ice wall melted, with water gushing down to the pavements below, but even so the massive bulk of its many glacial tons took several days to disappear.

The ice wall was a beautiful object, but also a powerful symbol, showing how defensive barriers could melt away completely, leaving no trace of conflict behind. To think of making such a symbolic artwork in this dramatic and historic setting required an extraordinarily creative mind; to actually carry it out required an extraordinarily determined personality and a large and skilled team of supporters. So, even if I had not known, I might have guessed that this was the work of Dale Chihuly.

The ice wall was the culmination of one of Chihuly's series of city exhibitions, which have taken place in locations as diverse as Venice, Jerusalem, and Monte Carlo. This time it was in the Tower of David, the forbidding fortress that has seen many of the great events in the tempestuous history of that city. It is now devoted to the history of Jerusalem, but this castle turned museum was transformed again by Chihuly's vast and colourful glass sculptures, juxtaposed with the venerable stones and making the viewer reassess both ancient and modern.

I had come to Jerusalem especially to see the exhibition and the ice wall project—and was not disappointed. At the V&A we had just agreed to install a 'Chandelier' by Chihuly in our front hall, and I wanted to witness at first hand the effect of his work. This was an important experience, because, while books and exhibition catalogues provide an invaluable record, they cannot convey the striking presence or the vibrant colours of the work itself. Nor can printed records fully demonstrate that interplay of old and new which is central to much of Chihuly's large-scale work. In due course our 'Chandelier' was created beneath the central dome of our entrance hall, to great public acclaim. It was the first major Chihuly work to be housed in the UK, and its success, combined with the huge popular interest in his work, convinced us that we should mount a major Chihuly exhibition as soon as possible. The results can be seen in the V&A show and are recorded in this book. This is powerful but accessible art, that can be viewed with pure pleasure but which can also convey a range of deeper meanings.

It is also, of course, particularly relevant to the V&A, with its wonderful historic collections of glass and its distinguished record of acquiring the best modern pieces. The juxtapositions here may not be as dramatic as the ice wall was in Jerusalem, but they are equally telling and equally beautiful.

Alan Borg · Director, Victoria and Albert Museum, 1995-2001

CHIHULY AT

THE V&A

Jennifer Hawkins Opie

Dale Chihuly is a phenomenon. His importance as a contemporary artist is unassailable, and his work has long been sought after by all major museums and galleries. But other issues about exhibiting his work also arise which are less often addressed in print. He has stepped far outside the normally enclosed parameters of glass. Such is his reputation that any major museum, especially one which counts glass among its core interests, must consider approaching the Chihuly organisation for a show of his work. Yet this is not done lightly. Chihuly himself, and his studio on his behalf, is highly demanding—and rightly so—in terms of display space and facilities, in publicity, presentation, and time. Their bargaining power is considerable, and a museum must be sure it can do him justice.

Significantly, Chihuly's glass—and the man himself—generates an excitement and a degree of attention that most other artists rarely approach. His glass is distinctive and grandly conceived, and his fame has been achieved through his growth as an artist as well as the overwhelming public response to his work. But he also carefully controls every facet of its presentation. The significance of this cannot be overestimated. Like every other material weighed down with the preconceptions of history but seeking to claim contemporary attention, glass needs ambassadors.

Chihuly's artistic success has its roots in a well-grounded academic and practical background and a progressive, consistent growth of ideas. A résumé of his career proves the point.

Born in 1941 in Tacoma, near Seattle, Washington, he is Hungarian, Czech, and Slavic on his father's side, Swedish and Norwegian on his mother's side. At the age of 17, he enrolled at the College of Puget Sound, where he wrote a term paper on Van Gogh and then re-designed his

Her Majesty The Queen and Dale Chihuly admiring the completed
V&A Chandelier at the opening of the exhibition 'A Grand Design';
October 1999

mother's recreation room, discovering in himself a response to colour and space. Chihuly transferred to the University of Washington in Seattle to study interior design and architecture in 1960, and the following year he learnt to melt and fuse glass—a start, but a very long way indeed from glassblowing. He also developed a lifelong passion for travelling.

For the next eight years he alternated between travelling in Ireland, Italy, Czechoslovakia, Germany, Sweden, Russia, and the Middle East and studying at the Universities of Washington and Wisconsin and at the Rhode Island School of Design. He earned three important degrees: a B.A. in interior design, a master's degree in sculpture, and another master's degree in ceramics. He also received two prestigious awards, a Louis C. Tiffany Foundation Grant and a Fulbright Fellowship to study abroad. These provided the opportunity to work and study with glass masters on the Venetian island of Murano. This was three years after he first blew glass, in 1965, an experience that had led him to study under the legendary Harvey Littleton, founder of the first studio glass course in America, at the University of Wisconsin.

Chihuly described his early fascination with his medium: 'I had this little studio in south Seattle . . . [where] I began to learn how glass melted and how you could fuse it together. One night I melted some stained glass between four bricks and put a pipe in there and gathered some glass and blew a bubble. . . . From that point on I wanted to be a glassblower. . . . I was totally infatuated, com-pletely absorbed in the concept of being a glassblower because to see this bubble come out at the end of this blowpipe [was] magical'.[i]

Tom Lind and Paula Stokes from the Chihuly Studio, installing the
V&A Chandelier in the museum's main entrance; October 1999

He had finally found his future. Hot glass and the thrill of blowing and manipulating it provided the drama, physical excitement, and camaraderie which have proved to be a lifelong passion.

Chihuly became a charismatic teacher, helped by his talent for establishing partnerships and appreciating and orchestrating parallel skills to his own. Two of his most important achievements were the establishment of the glass program at the Rhode Island School of Design in 1969 and co-founding the Pilchuck Glass School, the now famous international school and workshop which started life in 1971 as a rain-soaked, slug-ridden summer camp in woods fifty miles north of Seattle.

The success of Pilchuck, against daunting odds, more than illustrates Chihuly's truly significant role in shaping the development of glassmaking in the United States and internationally over the last thirty years. His well-honed practical skills, an essential creative energy, and sheer determination, combined with his flair for motivating others, refused all possibility of failure. It is hard to believe now that the earliest students had to build their own shelters and the hotshop from wood and materials found locally, and they made many of their own tools.

This was a time of discovery and new awareness of Native American beliefs, natural forces, and spiritual, environmental, and life-style concerns. All of these chimed with the establishment of the Pilchuck camp and the energies put into the skills necessary to make the glass. With hot glass still in its infancy as a studio medium, very few of the people there had much, if any, experience with glassmaking, and even fewer had any reliable technical expertise in terms of mixing and colouring glass. Even those who did, like Chihuly, chose to mix the raw ingredients themselves rather than buy ready-made and re-melted glass.

Chihuly has progressed from these years of an experimental, hippie-like existence to an international stardom which is phenomenal, but he has never stopped testing the boundaries of established glassmaking. By the 1990s, not only had he received numerous academic degrees and awards, but he could list more than 180 museums housing his works as part of their permanent collections, including the Museum of Modern Art and the Metropolitan Museum of Art, both in New York; the Musée des Arts Décoratifs, Palais du Louvre, Paris; the National Museum of Modern Art, Tokyo; and the Victoria and Albert Museum, London. His work has been shown in solo exhibitions across North and South America, Europe, the Middle East, the Far East, Australia, and New Zealand. His recent exhibition in Israel at the Tower of David Museum of the History of Jerusalem drew a record-breaking attendance of more than 1.2 million visitors in twelve months.

It is not just Chihuly's popularity and the recognition that he has revolutionized how glass is perceived as an art form which provide good reasons for museums to show his work. At the V&A, his work will have a special resonance. His 'oeuvre' owes much to the grand tradition of Venetian glass which this museum represents with international standing. Therefore, the museum offers a splendid context in which Chihuly's work may be seen within a historical continuum. The audience for Chihuly can move from his work in present-day Seattle to Venice in the 1960s and 1970s and then back to the Renaissance— the museum's collections demonstrate how the earlier glass and the techniques for making it inform Chihuly's glass. There is a natural symbiosis. Additionally, the V&A seeks to show the work of artists and designers who are the leaders in their field; who clearly have some thing to say; who challenge established perceptions. Material and technique are not enough. Physicality, intellect, and tension must be under-pinning the work to bring the promise of a rich, rewarding experience, engaging hearts and minds.

The importance of Chihuly's art both as material and as concept has been well examined by a number of writers. Most notably, critic Donald Kuspit, in his monograph on Chihuly, delivers an analysis which places the work squarely within the avant-garde. He writes that Chihuly, with ambitions (perhaps subliminal at first) to transform and deepen consciousness, must 'find transcendence in the medium itself. He must . . . mythologize glass into the ideal medium of expression'.[ii] Kuspit describes how Chihuly first used landscape as a point of departure at Pilchuck, where it was a vital part of the founding philosophy, and it has remained with him ever since. In the early 1970s, Chihuly was making environmental works in glass, neon, argon, and ice. These were large installations, as the titles suggest: 'Glass Forest' and '20,000 Pounds of Ice and Neon' (which covered six hundred square feet). These were serious attempts at the start of his career to engage with site specificity and performance, mediated by the opportunities and challenges of working with new materials. The materials were challenged and challenging, and the art demanded action and reaction. The ice melted, the glass was stretched, the audience was expected to enter the arena and experience the stridently artificial light. And as he became more intensely involved and skilled in the use of the medium, it was the glass which became all-important. He said later: 'I can sometimes switch over to neon, plastic or ice but only because they connect to the properties of glass . . . '.[iii] This was the first step along the way to mythologizing the material.

As has often been explained, perhaps the most valuable lesson Chihuly learned early on in Venice was the method of teamwork which he saw at the Venini factory on the island of Murano. Collaborative glassmaking in the form of a shared furnace and, probably, an interchangeable team was practised in Venice by the 16th century. By the 20th century, the teamwork Chihuly so admired was a long-established tradition. Three or four people work together in a choreographed performance—each playing a precise part in the gathering of the glass and the making of the object under the direction of the master gaffer, the 'maestro'. At this critical moment in his formative artistic development, Chihuly responded to the skilful manipulation of hot glass—the sheer thrill and physicality, the style, the panache with which Italian makers more than any other do the performance. There is surely no doubt that this aspect was as seductive to Chihuly as the glass itself. It is equally clear that the ripe forms, weighty or probing, now typical of his work convey a writhing sexuality which is very much to do with the way they are blown and manipulated.[iv] Ironically, it is probably the insistent physicality of Chihuly's glass that has led to some accusations of undisciplined opulence—implying intellectual carelessness. But this is where Chihuly is so often misunderstood, and unreasonably so. As he progressed through the great series of forms which are recognisable worldwide as Chihuly glass, each step along the way was grounded in his knowledge of other art forms and other cultures—from Native American blankets and basketry to Japanese ikebana and Venetian art glass of the 1920s and 1930s. His work has become more tender, more expressive, and more frenzied by turns. Once he had made the move from his earliest vessels, the 'Cylinders', to the far more organic 'Baskets', these led on to a wealth of ripe, quivering shapes, subtly textured and coloured. He said, 'In the summer of 1977 I was visiting the Tacoma Historical Society . . . and I remember being struck by a pile of Northwest Coast Indian baskets that were stacked one inside the other. They were dented and misshapen, wonderful forms. I don't really know what made me want to reproduce them in glass, but that was my mission for the summer'.[v] Chihuly was searching for forms and for a means of expressive power. His glass 'Baskets' were shown in groups, stacked one inside the other. They became an environment into which an audience might be drawn, within which, if succumbed to, there was the power to alter consciousness.

The point at which Chihuly's work moved from baskets in glass to the more purely abstract was when he began the series now known as 'Seaforms'—a name attached to them later because of their resemblance to sea creatures like anemones. In the 'Macchia' series, begun in 1981, he experimented with a force which moved well beyond the gentle, somnolent beauty of the earlier works. He had moved away from the specific to the abstract, transforming the subject matter into an exploration of a different world. Textures and colours became more fearless and more challenging. Decoration, so often nervously avoided by others, became not only acceptable in his hands but a vocabulary with which he was skilful enough to manipulate an ever-widening range of emotions. After 'Macchia' came 'Persians', 'Venetians', 'Ikebana', 'Putti', 'Niijima Floats', 'Chandeliers', and the increasingly ambitious environmental installations of 'Towers', 'Reeds', 'Pergolas', 'Windows', and 'Ceilings'.

The V&A had been considering an approach to Chihuly for some years. There are three works by him in the permanent collections, but the museum had not taken the further step of engaging with Chihuly the environmental artist. In 1999, an invitation was formally extended. Practically, the museum wanted a major, unambiguous statement for its main entrance which would confirm the museum's commitment to contemporary art and design. The space and its use at the time suggested a chandelier, and although glass was not essential, no other artist offered the same overwhelming ability to think on the required scale and with the essential imaginative leap. The museum was aware that Chihuly is a rare and unquestionable mix of artist and advocate, a man of complex and curious intellect. It was also aware that the glass which results often challenges but is never irrelevant. And it was this that the museum anticipated with relish.

The sculpture, originally titled 'Ice Blue and Spring Green Chandelier' but now officially known as the 'V&A Chandelier', was designed, blown, and first assembled in Seattle. Over a period of seven months, negotiations and discussions filled the electronic airways, the museum's roof was strengthened, and a new chain was ordered. Finally, the 'Chandelier' was hung in the dome area of the main entrance to the museum in October 1999, to coincide with the opening of the exhibition 'A Grand Design'. The installation, by a team of three from the Chihuly Studio, took place over a period of four days and was a public event in itself. 'A Grand Design', which had travelled to five venues in North America over the previous two years, explored the history of the museum's collecting from its foundation to the present day. Chihuly's 'Chandelier', therefore, celebrated the latest, most contemporary finale to the show. The opening of the exhibition and the 'Chandelier' was marked by a visit by Her Majesty The Queen and His Royal Highness The Duke of Edinburgh.

The 'V&A Chandelier' was the latest in a series of such works, begun in 1992, for which the title 'Chandelier' is something of a misnomer. The works are suspended sculptures, externally or occasionally internally lit, and using the Venetian 18th-century chandelier form merely as a departure point. In Chihuly's hands the form has become a massive artwork, changing the character of the main entrance. The 'V&A Chandelier' presents the newly arrived visitor with an unmistakable contemporary statement, and the interest it generates is obvious. Arriving visitors

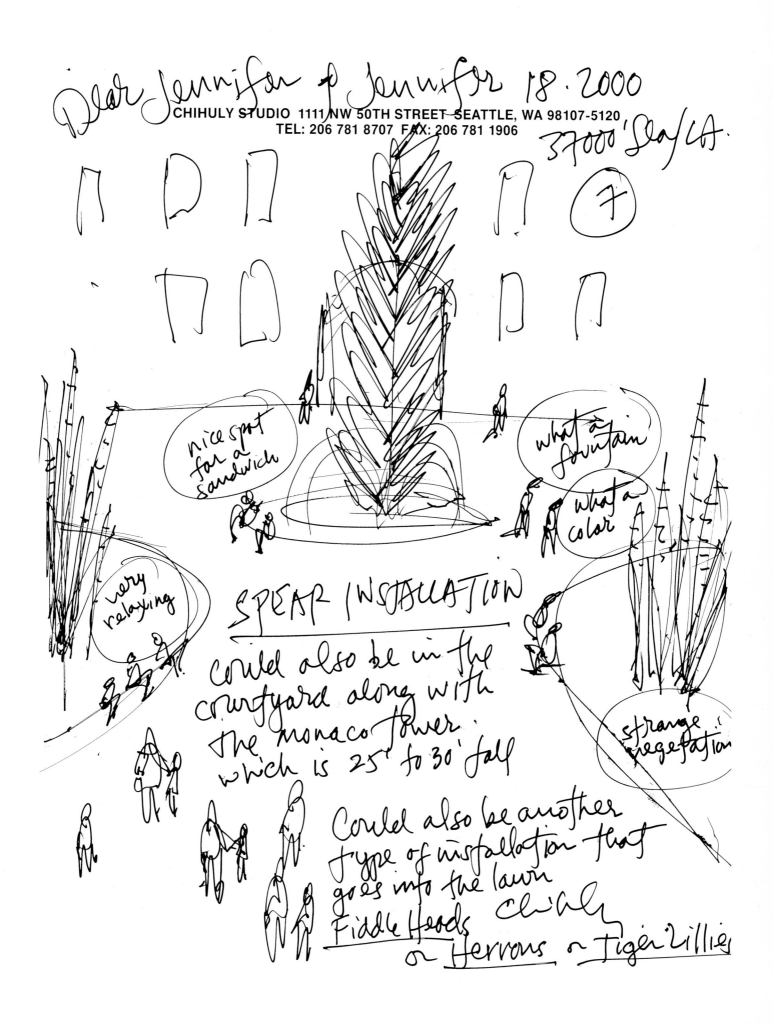

stop, stare, and take out their cameras. As a reminder of their visit, it is certainly the most photographed single object in the museum. The British press, faced with glass on a scale and of an impact which was previously unheard of in the UK, oscillated between uncertainty and superlatives: 'rather wonderful . . . a fantastical creation' ('The Times')[vi]; 'whether it attracts you or appalls you, Chihuly's work is certainly breathtaking' (London's 'Evening Standard')[vii]; 'a dazzling modern commission' ('Crafts')[viii]; 'Wriggling like a large and glowing creature of the sea, this spectacularly weird glass chandelier . . . [is] the first time Dale's work has been seen on this scale in the UK and he seems sure to gather a few more admirers as a result' ('Homes and Interiors')[ix]; 'the work of Seattle glass artist Dale Chihuly is breathtaking—as those who have seen his vast, colourful chandelier newly hung in the V&A Museum will know' ('idFX').[x]

The critical success of the 'Chandelier' encouraged the V&A to pursue its long-held interest in staging an extended Chihuly exhibition in the form of an 'intervention' throughout the ground floor of the museum and out into the courtyard garden. This exhibition, 'Chihuly at the V&A', will be opened to the public on 21 June 2001 for a period of four months, an unusually long run for the museum. Beginning at the perimeter of the dome area in the main entrance, in a space which is visible through the outside doors to passers-by on the pavement beyond, the powerfully colourful 'Orange Basket Forest' acts as an introduction. Recognising the changes made to the area since its installation and the consequent alteration to the architectural balance, Chihuly has extended the 'Chandelier' in length. Descending the steps into the gallery housing the museum's internationally renowned medieval collections, the exhibition continues with displays of many of Chihuly's glass series: 'Baskets', 'Seaforms', 'Persians', 'Venetians', 'Ikebana', 'Putti', 'Jerusalem Cylinders', 'Macchia', and, overhead, a 'Persian Ceiling'. This uniquely Chihuly concept allows the visitor to walk below a sumptuously coloured assemblage of glass, bathed in the filtered light of a richly experiential, consciousness-altering space. The visual contrast between Chihuly's glass and the medieval treasures in ivory, enamel, silver, and gold beneath German and French stained glass in the surrounding gallery multiplies the experience. Outside the glass display, the exhibition also shows Chihuly's energetic and richly informative drawings, the most important means by which he communicates his ideas to the glassblowing team. Emerging into the Renaissance gallery, the visitor is met by a 'Macchia Forest'. A group of richly colourful and dramatically textured 'Macchia' forms displayed at eye level envelops and enriches the senses even further. Beyond, into the garden, installations of experimental forms lead directly to a nine-metre-high (thirty-foot) 'Tower of Light' over the fountain. And, to add to the intensity of the visual display, all of the courtyard installations are seen directly in front of the museum's original 1860s entrance, with its decorated architectural terra-cotta as a backdrop.

The experience of working with Chihuly and the Chihuly Studio has been demanding but rewarding. Chihuly remains the energetic, charismatic artist in whom the free-wheeling student and young teacher with boundless vision are still recognisable, yet he is also now the head of a major studio and a businessman. This metamorphosis is central to understanding Chihuly the man, but it was also the result of one specific event. Chihuly no longer makes the glass himself. A very serious car accident in 1976 deprived him of the sight in one eye, altering his perception of depth. Since then he has become more the conductor of the orchestra, rather than soloist or lead violin in the actual blowing sessions. In many ways this role has freed him. He understands glass entirely, and indeed his early works demonstrate a rare and sensitive skill which now he conveys by drawing, teaching, and engaging directly with the glassblowers as they are working. He will often be there, on the workshop floor, closely orchestrating the performance and demonstrating his own engagement through the media of paint and drawing. But it is equally true that he has no need to be there throughout the making and so he is free to travel, to spread the gospel of glass and constantly to recharge the batteries which keep him always driving forward. His team of makers, most of them artists in their own right, is fully in tune with his ideas and is able to do much of the work without his presence. For his part, Chihuly has developed more systematic ways of working with the studio. Were it necessary for him to be there in the glass workshop daily, perhaps he might never have become the artist and international celebrity he is now. Nevertheless, despite being one step removed from the process, he has said: 'Glass has satisfied my need to really understand the material that I am working with and to comprehend and exploit its unique properties of light and transparency. . . . I need to be assured that I've mastered a medium or material, and glass is the only one that I feel completely at ease in'.[xi] His oneness with the material has produced supreme results and transformed perceptions about his chosen art form.

Dale Chihuly is one of the most honoured and creative contemporary sculptors in glass. The Victoria and Albert Museum is a fitting site to bring the work of this extraordinary artist to an even broader audience.

i Oldknow, Tina, 'Pilchuck: A Glass School', University of Washington, Seattle, and Pilchuck Glass School, p. 38

ii Kuspit, Donald, 'Chihuly', Portland Press, 1998, p. 33

iii Oldknow, Tina, 'Pilchuck: A Glass School', p. 23

iv 'Chihuly Over Venice', video, '. . . is that sexual or not!'

v Chihuly, 'Color, Glass and Form', Kodansha International, 1986, pp. 19–20

vi 'The Times', 13 August 1999

vii 'Evening Standard', 8 December 1999

viii 'Crafts', Jan./Feb. 2000

ix 'Homes and Interiors', No. 14, 1999

x 'idFX and FX International', December 1999

xi Oldknow, interview with Chihuly in 'Pilchuck: A Glass School', p. 23

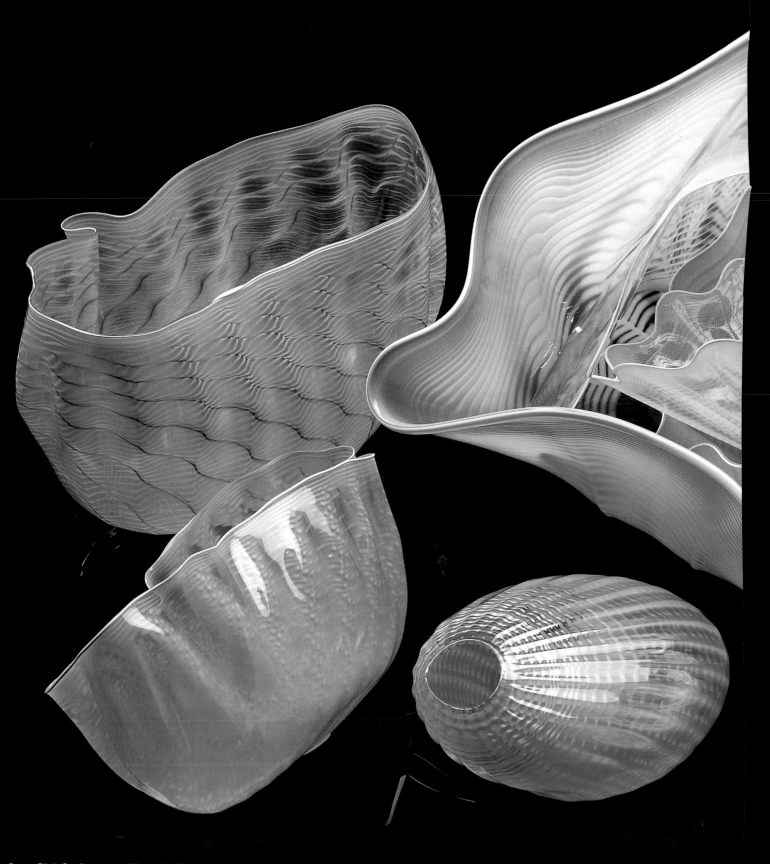

Dawn Pink Seaform with White Lip Wrap, 1981
9 x 17 x 9"

Pink Seaform with White Lip Wrap, 1980
8 x 12 x 5"

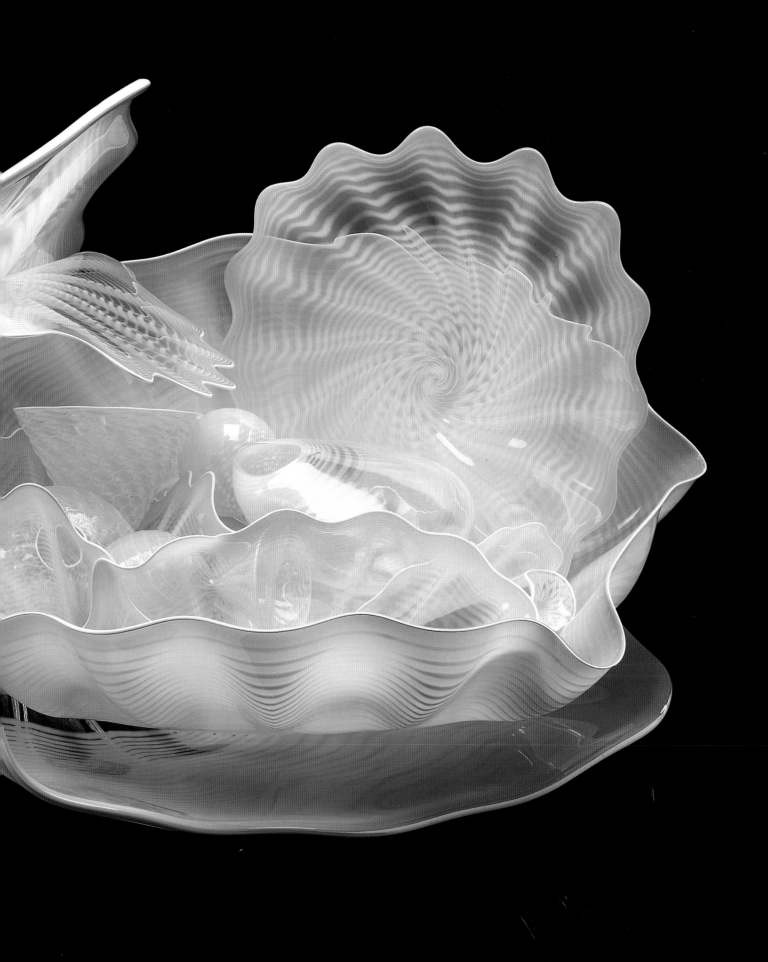

< **Pale Pink Seaform,** 1981
5 x 9 x 7"

Cameo Pink Seaform Set with White Lip Wraps, 1989
18 x 34 x 29"

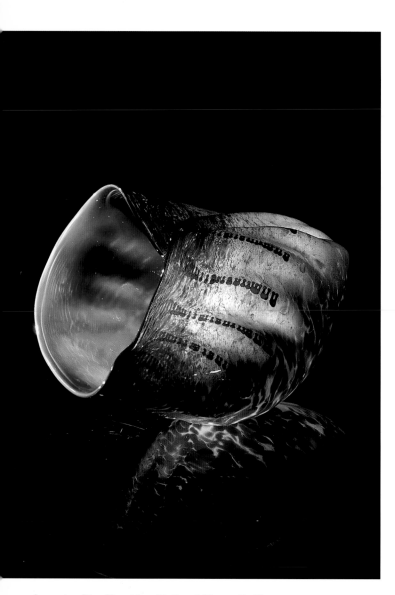

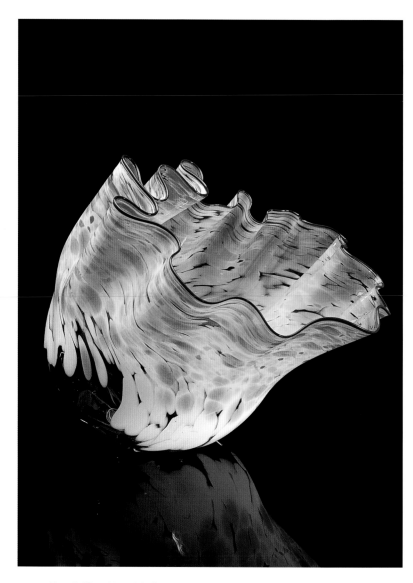

Armenian Blue Macchia with Burnt Sienna Lip Wrap, 1981
4 x 8 x 7"

Peach Macchia with Cobalt Lip Wrap, 1985
17 x 18 x 21"

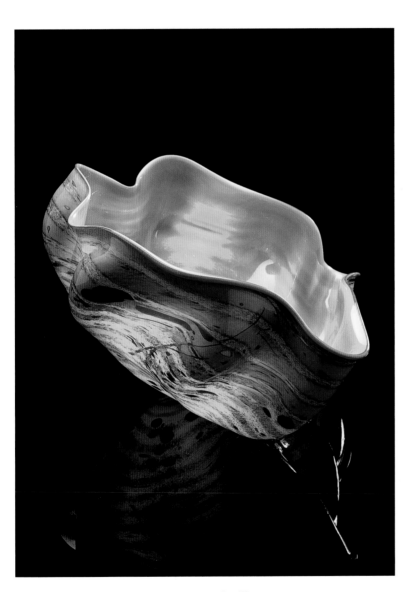

Chartreuse Macchia with Tangerine Lip Wrap, 1983
6 x 11 x 10"

Dust Gray Macchia with Cobalt Lip Wrap, 1992
15 x 16 x 17"

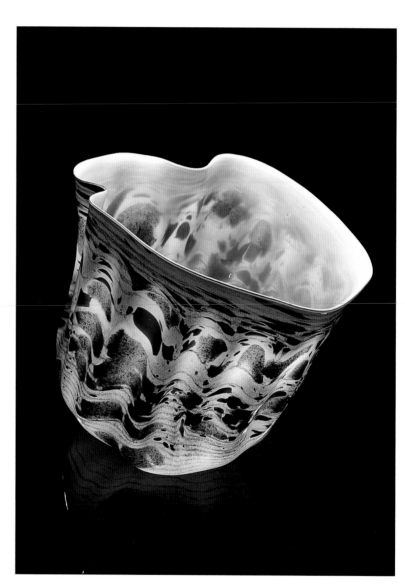

Algonquin Orange Macchia, 1991
5 x 12 x 10"

Bisque Macchia with Colonial Yellow Lip Wrap, 1982
10 x 12 x 13"

Tabac Macchia with Light Blue Lip Wrap, 1982
8 x 11 x 10"

White and Chestnut Macchia, 1982
6 x 7 x 9"

Leopard Spot Basket Set with Chrome Yellow Lip Wraps, 1992
10 x 21 x 14"

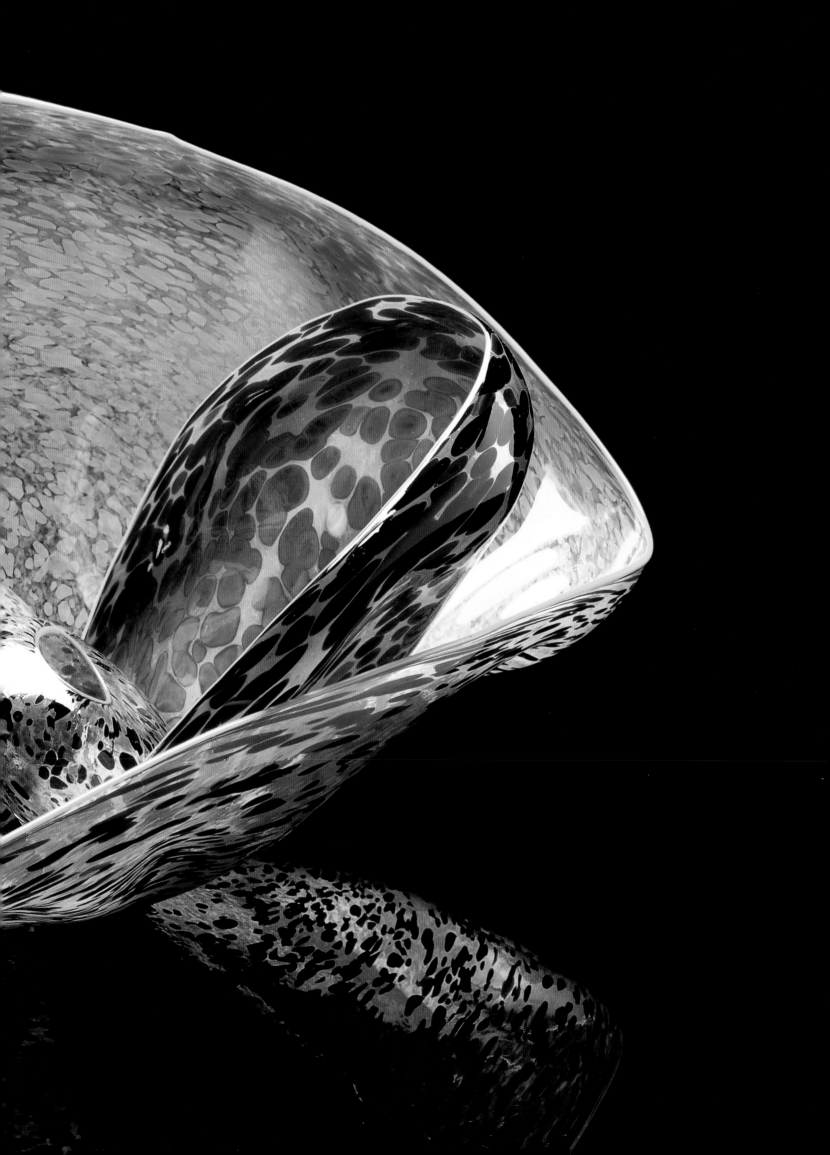

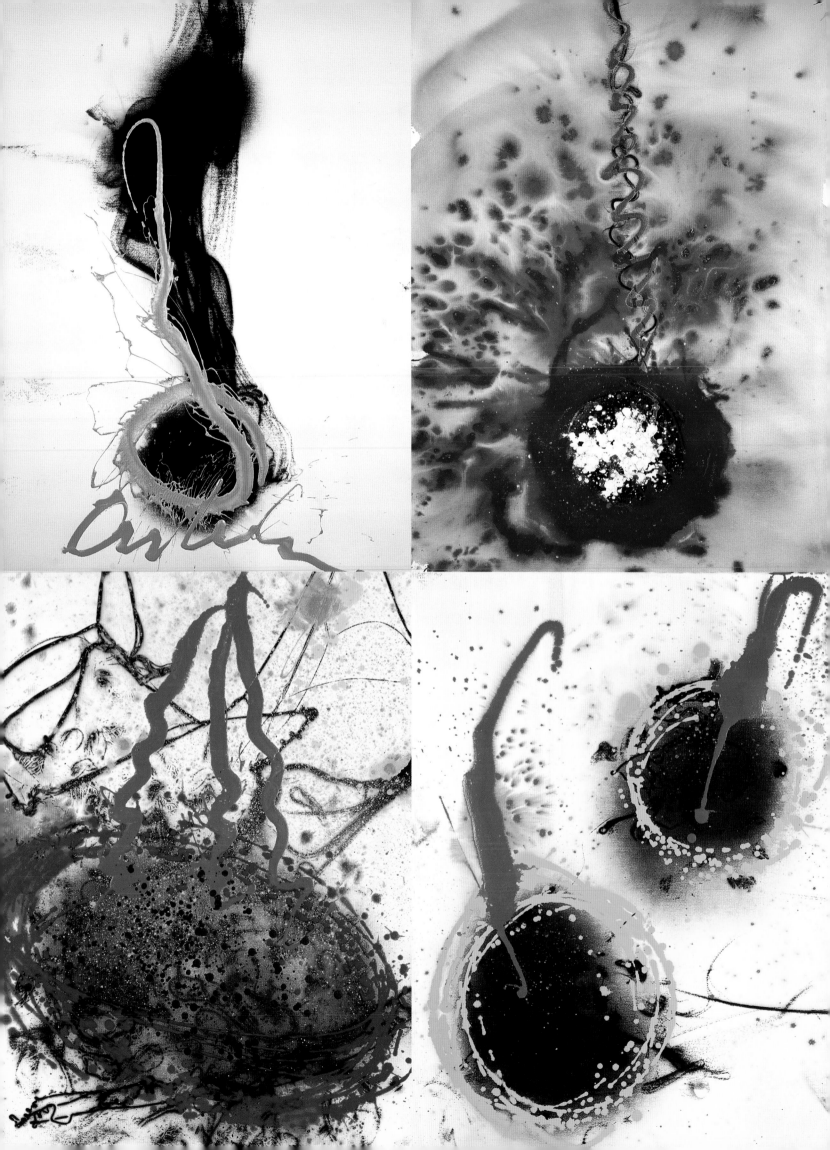

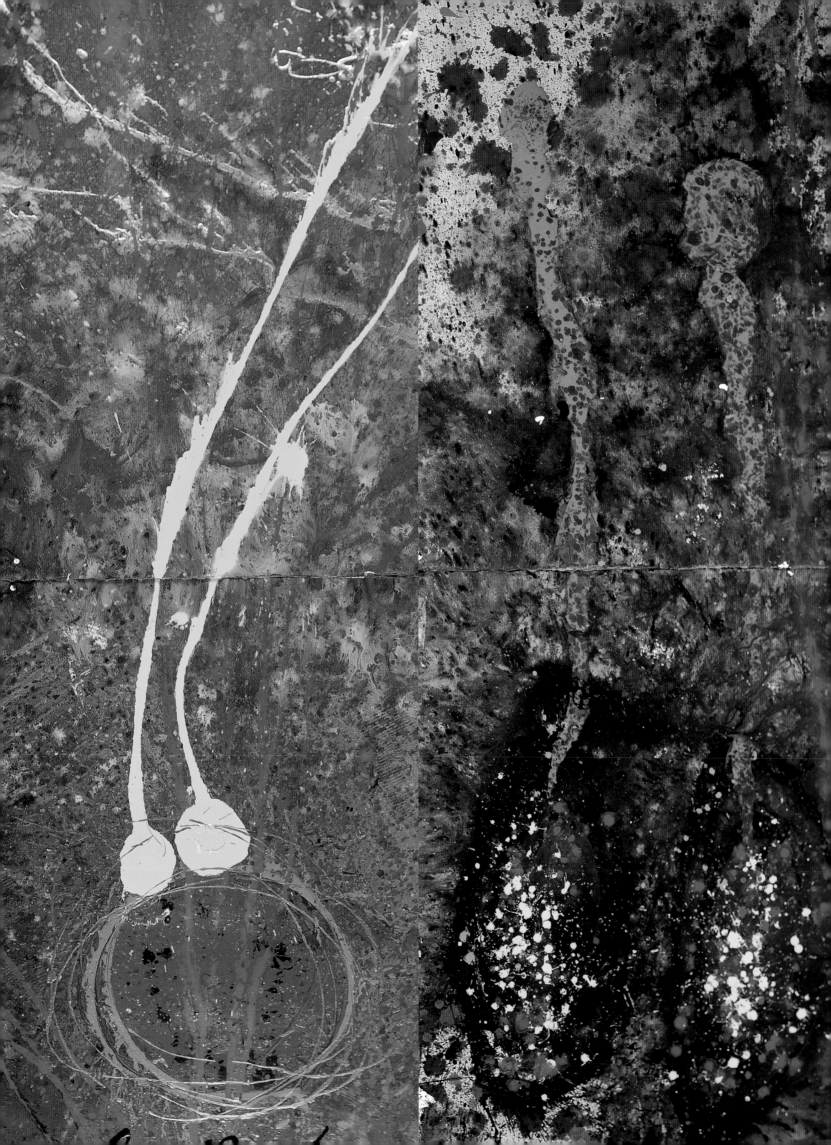

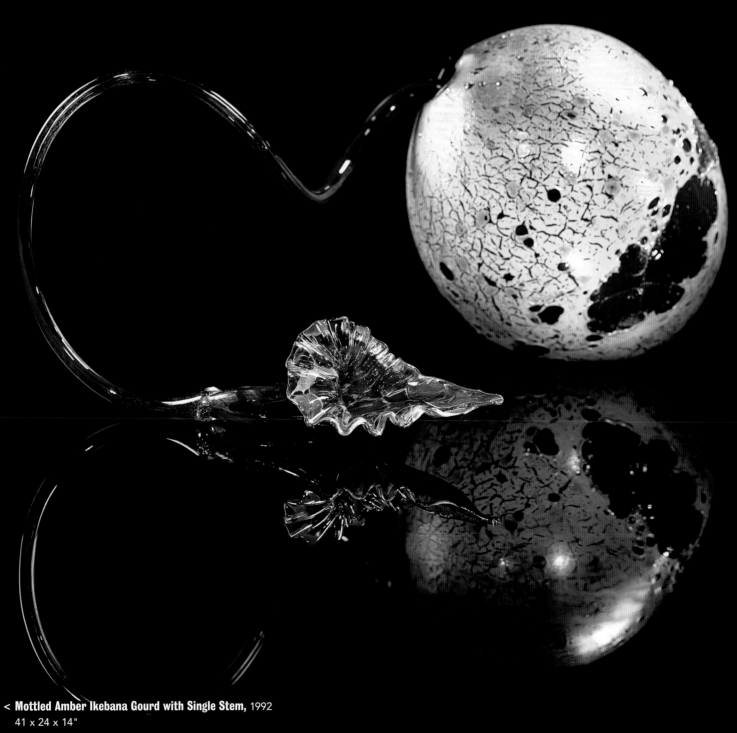

< **Mottled Amber Ikebana Gourd with Single Stem,** 1992
41 x 24 x 14"

May Green Ikebana with Royal Lily Stem, 1992
39 x 22 x 18"

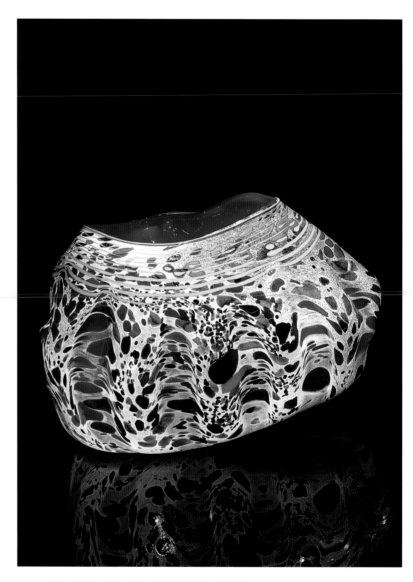

Kyoto Orange Macchia with Tar Lip Wrap, 1982
13 x 9 x 9"

Royal Blue Macchia with Pale Olive Lip Wrap, 1982
9 x 15 x 12"

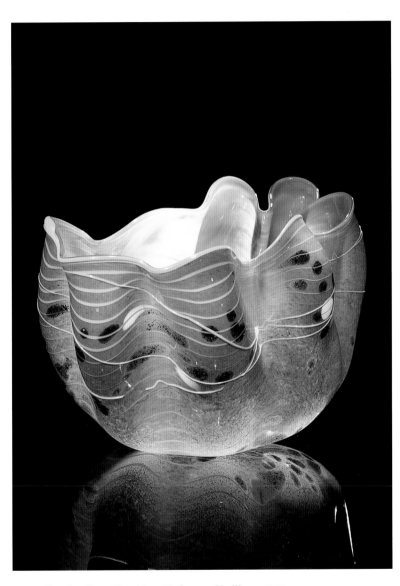

Russian Gray Macchia with Canary Lip Wrap, 1982
5 x 8 x 5"

Pumpkin Macchia with Olive Lip Wrap, 1982
5 x 7 x 7"

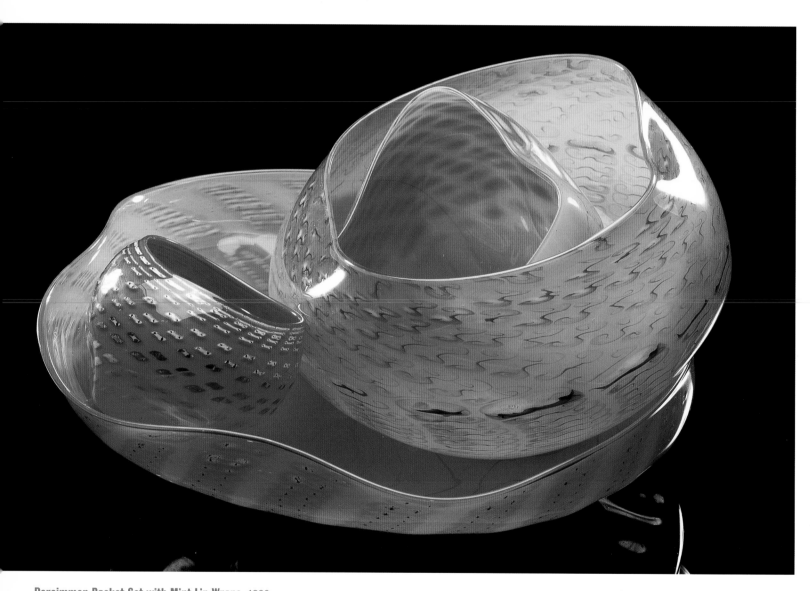

Persimmon Basket Set with Mint Lip Wraps, 1980
7 x 13 x 12"

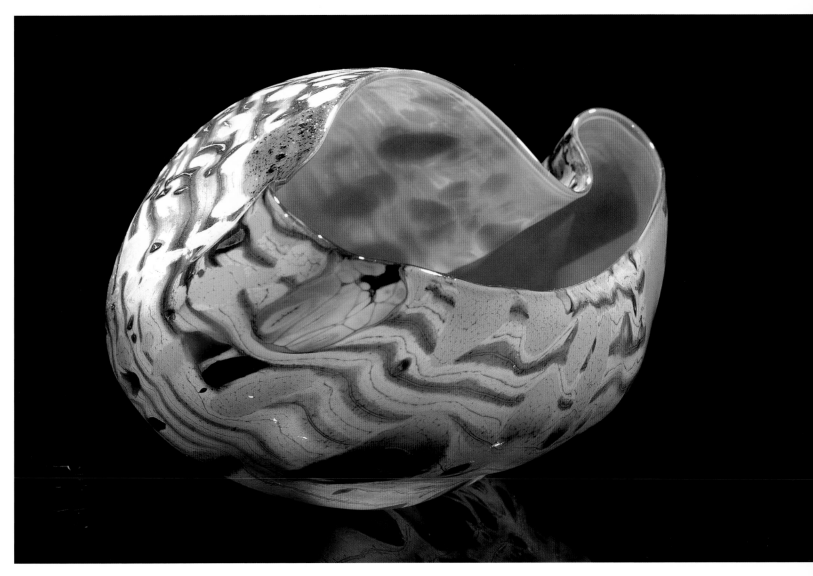

Burnt Orange Macchia, 1982
3 x 5 x 5"

Orange Ochre Persian Set with Black Lip Wraps, 1989
19 x 32 x 19"

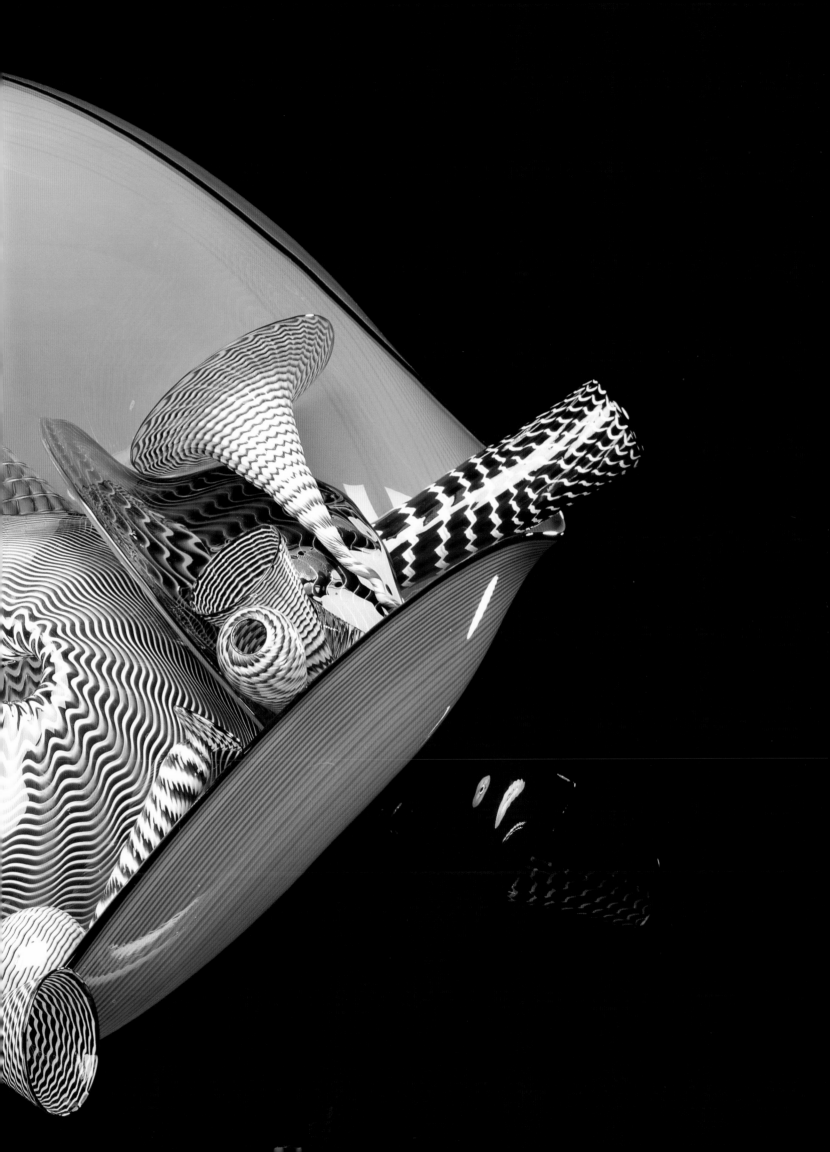

Lime Persian Set with Rhodonite Lip Wraps, 1988
6 x 14 x 12"

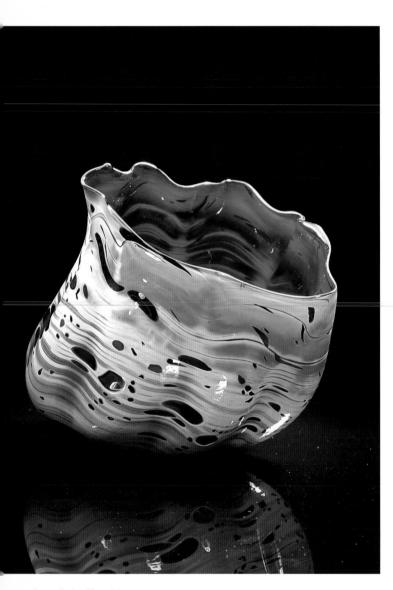

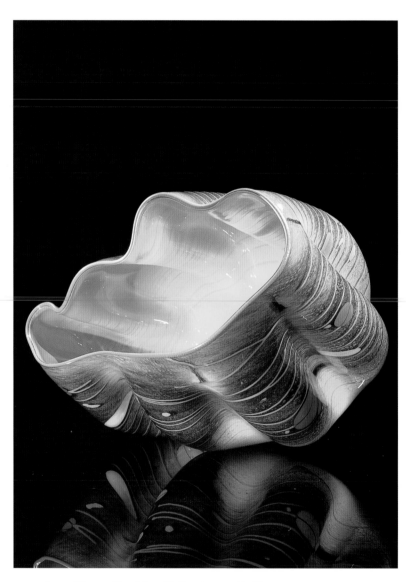

Deep Ruby Macchia, 1981
5 x 5 x 6"

Laurel Green Macchia with Persimmon Lip Wrap, 1981
5 x 7 x 6"

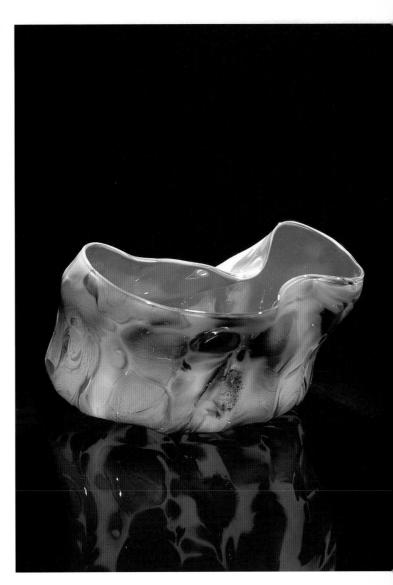

Mazarine Blue Macchia with Spanish Red Lip Wrap, 1981
6 x 6 x 7"

Paramount Blue Macchia, 1982
3 x 5 x 5"

Astral White and Aurora Pink Seaform Set, 2001
31 x 86 x 40"

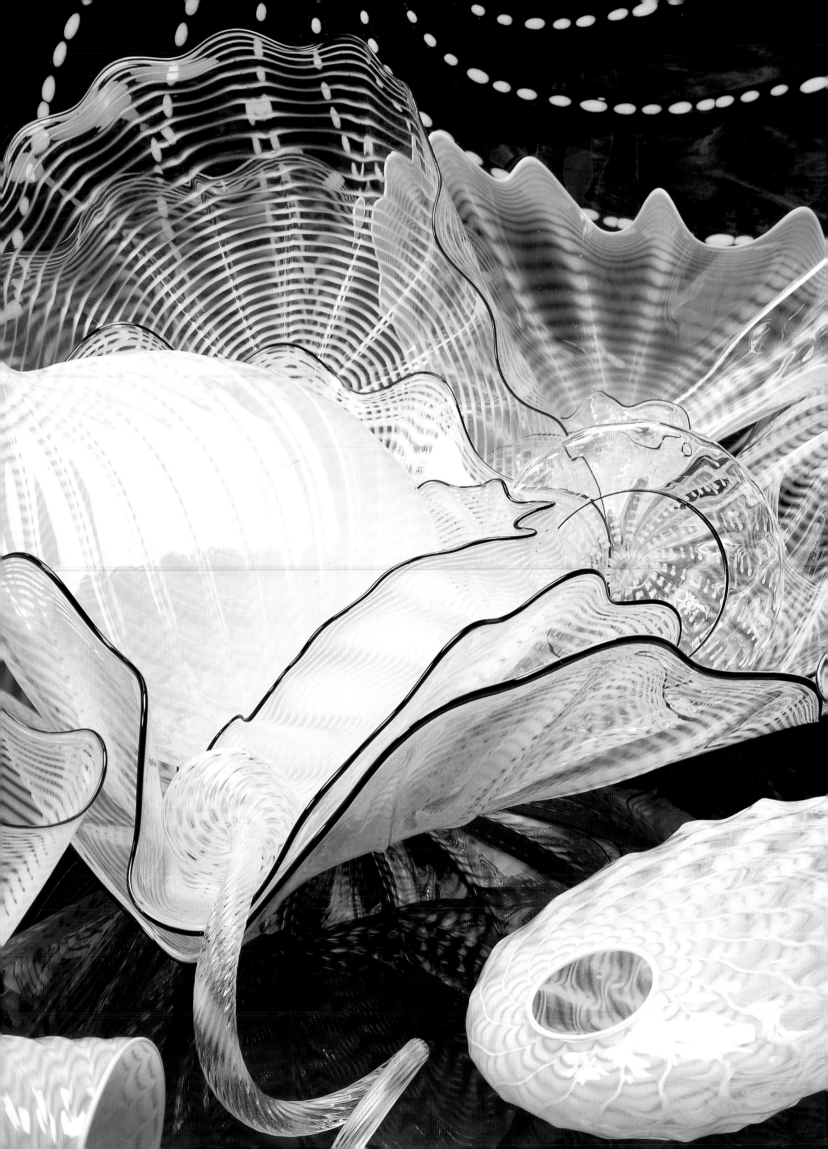

VENETIAN

TRADITION

Reino Liefkes

Goblet, colourless, opaque red and white glass, blown, mould-blown,
and tooled. Made in Venice, ca. 1700, H. 26.0 cm (10¼").
Victoria & Albert Museum, inv. 108-1853

Glassmaking in Venice has an immensely rich history. From the 15th century onwards, the name of the small glassmakers' island of Murano has been virtually synonymous with glasswares of the finest and most sophisticated kind.

Venetian glassmaking has its roots in the great Roman glass traditions on the nearby mainland. Archaeological evidence from the 7th century points at the production of coloured glass 'tesserae' or cubes used for wall mosaics on the island of Torcello, and references to glassmakers dating from the 10th century onwards can be found in the Venetian archives.

A breakthrough for Venice as an aspiring trading nation came in 1204, when the crusaders used Venetian ships to sail to Constantinople and sack the city. As a form of payment, the Venetians claimed the treasures looted from the city, parts of which can still be seen in the treasury of St. Mark's Basilica. But their greatest gain was in the resulting economic changes, as from that time onwards Venice dominated the Mediterranean trade in luxury goods from the East.

The council of the city also made serious efforts to establish its own production of luxury goods, especially textiles and glass, and there is evidence that Byzantine craftsmen were brought in to help achieve this. The glass industry became heavily regulated by the Guild of Glassmakers. The first set of statutes governing glassmakers, the famous 'Capitulare de Fiolaris', dates from 1271. This contains rules and regulations for all those involved in glassmaking, from furnace owners to the youngest apprentices, all of whom were by now organised in the Guild of Glassmakers. The 'Capitulare' was regularly updated and amended until the last version was issued in 1776.

These documents, together with others in the Venetian archives, provide a vivid insight into the way in which the guild deliberately developed a highly organised industry, one geared towards export markets and striving for a worldwide monopoly. The guild encouraged technical developments by providing additional trade benefits and dispensations for their inventors. Once established and proven successful, new techniques became jealously guarded trade secrets. Glass-recipe books, containing glassmakers' families' secret formulae, were treasured and closely guarded. Handed down from father to son, they were regularly annotated with new or refined recipes and other discoveries. As the success of Venetian glass was to a large extent based on the careful selection and purification of raw materials, the export of these materials was either forbidden or heavily restricted. Most importantly, the glassmakers themselves were not allowed to practice their art outside Murano, and they could be heavily punished if they were caught doing so. Not only the deserters, but also the families they left behind, could face fines, imprisonment, or the galleys. We know of one case in which the inquisitors of the guild threatened to use a hired assassin. The concentration of all glass furnaces on the nearby island of Murano to reduce the risk of fires in Venice, which was the result of a decree of 1291, also facilitated control over the glassmakers' community.

One of the most important innovations around 1450 was the development of an extremely pure and clear type of colourless glass called 'cristallo', which was to become the 'trade mark' of Venetian glass. Named after naturally occurring rock crystal, this could be blown very thinly and tooled into the most intricate shapes. 'Cristallo' laid the foundation for many other great developments of the 15th and 16th centuries, both in glassmaking techniques and in the opening up of a new repertoire of shapes and object types.

All these protective measures and technical and stylistic developments led to complete international dominance by the Venetian style of glassmaking. The finest glass of Venice found its way to the courts and the tables of the nobility and wealthy merchants across Europe. Such was the demand for Venetian glass that an exodus of Venetian glassmakers was inevitable. Generous payments and favourable conditions provided enough incentive for the Italians to risk the guild's wrath and set up workshops abroad. From the mid-16th century onwards, numerous Venetian glass-houses sprang up in the Netherlands, France, Germany, England, and other countries. There, Venetian glassmakers produced Venetian-style glass using raw materials which were as close a match as possible to the ones they used at home. The term for the glass they made, 'à la façon de Venise' (in the Venetian manner), was already in use by the middle of the 16th century. Depending on local demands, they often adapted their style and used indigenous shapes and vessel-types.

As most of the 'façon de Venise' glass-houses were high-profile business enterprises, requiring substantial investments, there are many accounts relating to their operation. Often contracts with the Italian glassmakers stipulated that they should train local youths to become skilled glassmakers. In many cases, this led to fruitful collaboration. We know of frequent instances of Italian glassmakers marrying furnace owners' daughters, thus consolidating business alliances. But it is easy to imagine that there were also many frictions caused by the clash between different cultural backgrounds, perhaps fuelled by the heat of the furnace and the huge quantities of beer that glassmakers often drank to withstand prolonged exposure to such high temperatures.

The great period of bloom of glassmaking in the Venetian style lasted until the late 17th century, when such refined

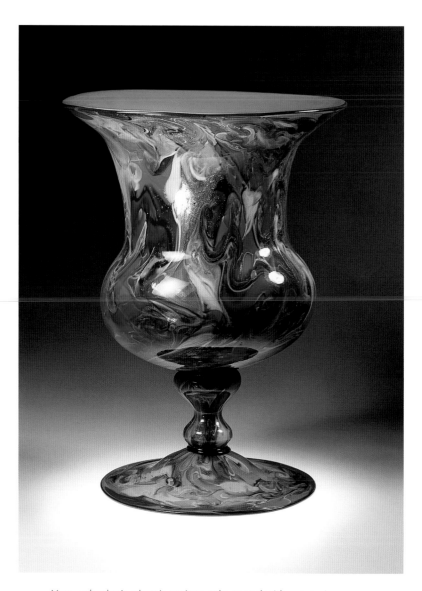

Vase, clear green glass, blown, with hot-worked and trailed decoration. Made in southern Spain, late 16th to 17th century, H. 19.7 cm (7¾"). Victoria & Albert Museum, inv. 151-1873

Vase, calcedonio glass in various colours and with aventurine inclusions. Made by Salviati & C., Murano, Venice, ca. 1868, H. 44.8 cm (17⅝"). Victoria & Albert Museum, inv. 904-1868

Design for a 'trionfo da tàvola' by Stefano Della Bella, pen and brown ink over black crayon on paper. Made in Italy (Florence), 1650–75, 34.4 cm x 26.0 cm (13⁹/₁₆ x 10¼"). Collection Gabinetto Disegni e Stampe, Uffici, Florence, inv. 999 ORN

Goblet, colourless and clear turquoise-blue glass, blown in an optic mould, with applied threads. Made in Venice, ca. 1575–1650, H. 21.0 cm (8¼"). Victoria & Albert Museum, inv. 5507-1859

fragility was no longer fashionable. In Venice itself, glass-makers were not very successful at imitating the new types of much heavier glass from England and central Europe. The sturdy simple shapes and the engraved decorations that were now rapidly becoming popular did not suit the Venetian glassmakers, and a sharp decline in the industry set in. The only wholly successful and original Venetian products of the 18th century were exuberantly ornate and colourful chandeliers. The situation worsened after Venice was occupied by the French in 1797 and after Napoleon abolished the Guild of Glassmakers in 1805. A full-scale revival of the industry in the second half of the 19th century was largely fuelled by the growing antiquarian interest from tourists, collectors, and design reformers. Glassmakers re-learned lost techniques and took inspiration from the past at the glass museum at Murano, which opened in 1861. The industry employed chemists to develop new kinds of glass with dazzling new colours. The resulting products may now be considered by many to be over-ornate and top-heavy, and even a caricature of earlier Venetian styles, but with their vibrant colours and exuberant theatrical design they laid the foundation for the re-development of technical virtuosity on which all later developments are based.

For the past seven centuries, the tiny island of Murano has been completely dominated by glassmaking. To anyone walking around its canals now, and visiting the countless glass factories, this sense of history is tangible. Many glassmakers of today are direct descendants of the great masters of the 15th century. The essence of glassmaking on Murano has always been a thorough understanding of the material and a complete reliance on hot-working techniques. Everything is made in the heat of the roaring furnace, in an atmosphere where every movement is orchestrated and perfect timing is essential. Masters have to start working at the furnace at a very early age to learn the secrets and techniques, the skills and tricks that have been passed on in their families for hundreds of years. But it is also crucial that they learn how to operate as part of the small team of makers around the master's chair.

It is likely that the medieval glassmaker worked more or less alone on the beakers and bottles he produced. A rare surviving picture of a 16th-century glass-house in Florence, which was set up and operated solely by Venetian glassmakers, gives us a glimpse of a more advanced way of working. The master glassmakers, who would have been responsible for most of the important stages in the process, sit on simple three-legged stools at one of the 'mouths' of the furnace. Through these openings they could reach the molten glass inside, but the openings were also used for re-heating the glass at various stages of the process of blowing and tooling. To the right of each of the seated masters in the painting can be seen a standing figure of a glassblower. These are almost certainly their assistants, who would have blown separate parts of the object and handed them to the master at precisely the moment he needed them. Every master had access to his own opening to the annealing chamber at the top of the furnace. The finished hot objects were placed in this chamber to cool gradually, thus preventing them from breaking. In the 17th century, the invention of the glassmaker's 'chair' or 'bench' as we know it today, with long slightly sloping supports to roll the blowpipe, was a step further in the specialisation of the team. The glassmaker would from now on remain seated most of the time, performing only the most difficult procedures that required the highest levels of skill. This makes perfect economic sense, as none of his valuable time was wasted. Obviously, the degree of complexity and size of the objects produced have always determined the exact size of the team.

Giovanni Maria Butteri, detail of an oil painting on panel. Made for
the Studiolo of the Grand Duke Francesco de' Medici in the Palazzo
Vecchio in Florence and still in situ, 1570–75

In Murano, the technical bravura of the master often goes hand in hand with an inherent sense of the theatrical. Through the ages, a visit to the glass factory has been a standard item on the itinerary of the foreign visitor to Venice, and this might well have encouraged the glass-makers to perform their skill with even greater flair. But the best glass-houses are usually well off the beaten track, allowing the masters to concentrate wholly on their work. The traditional Venetian techniques almost all rely on advanced hot-working skills. One of the few exceptions to this was the technique of enamelling, which was largely abandoned after the early 16th century. Other techniques, such as 'chalcedonio', 'millefiori', and filigree glass, all involve creating decorative effects incorporated in the material itself. These techniques rely heavily on the technical knowledge and experience as well as the skill of the glassmakers. During the latter part of the 16th and the 17th centuries, new shapes and new types of vessels were introduced. The glassmakers used predominantly colourless 'cristallo', often adding a single clear blue glass trail to emphasise the shape. While they continued to make quite simple-shaped glasses with flowing lines, there was also a tendency towards more complex designs. The most complex objects were designed by artists and were probably intended for special banquet feasts. Technically, these combined mould-blowing and manipulating at the 'mouth' of the furnace (also called the glory hole) with intricate 'lamp-worked' details, blown from the thinnest, prefabricated tubes over an oil or paraffin flame which was powered by foot-operated bellows. Such complicated follies were probably not intended to last, and indeed, unfortunately, only design drawings and a few fragments have survived.

Although the quality of craftsmanship suffered during the period of decline in the 18th century, the sense of theatricality and the exuberance of colours and shapes were further explored. The same is true for the revival glass of the 19th and early 20th centuries. Modernism arrived relatively late in Murano. In the 1920s, designers began to look back at the simplicity of form of the early Renaissance, using subtle monochrome colours. In the 1950s and 1960s, Italian design became a dominant international force, and Venetian glass was very much part of this. Designers of international calibre, working in close relationship with the best masters of Murano, went back to the roots of Venetian glassmaking. The best designers and masters used traditional Venetian techniques, such as filigree and 'millefiori', in innovative and stimulating ways. Today, technical virtuosity has again become a hallmark of the glassmakers of Murano. This can be observed equally well in their highly artistic products and in their more standard repertoire, and is even a feature of the best wares produced for tourists. Many of the best masters have specialised and have become particularly accomplished in one particular technique or way of working. Again, the tradition of passing skills on in a closed and concentrated environment, from generation to generation, has produced the most wonderful fruits. Murano now has specialised glassblowers, makers of filigree glass, and sculptors in hot glass, all of whom rank among the very best in the world. Nowhere in the world can we find such technical skill, combined with understanding of the material, as in this small island off the Adriatic coast. But there is a real danger of artistic inbreeding in this tiny community. This is not helped by the fact that the glassmakers of Murano cannot even produce enough to supply their tourist market, a consumer group which does not demand artistic innovation. It is of paramount importance that the best masters challenge and renew themselves continually.

This can be done only by looking beyond the direct horizon, just as their predecessors did. It is vital that the masters travel to work abroad and also welcome foreign artists into their workshops. This is exactly how the industry prospered in the golden age of the 15th to 17th century.

Chihuly was one of the first modern foreign artists working in glass to come to Venice, and he was lucky to work with some of the world's best masters. Many contemporary glass-artists have abandoned blowing for other production methods, but for Chihuly blowing and manipulating hot glass are the quintessential glassmaking techniques. The main attraction of Venice was that he could engage with the most experienced teams of highly skilled glassblowers. But the process was entirely reciprocal; Chihuly has brought to Venice a new way of thinking and new ideas about scale and meaning of works of art, which have had an enormous impact on the masters with whom he works.

What is so special about Chihuly's collaboration with Venetian masters such as Pino Signoretto and Lino Tagliapietra is that the ideas and technical abilities are compatible and complement each other so well. In both cases, this has led to the creation of something truly wonderful and unique.

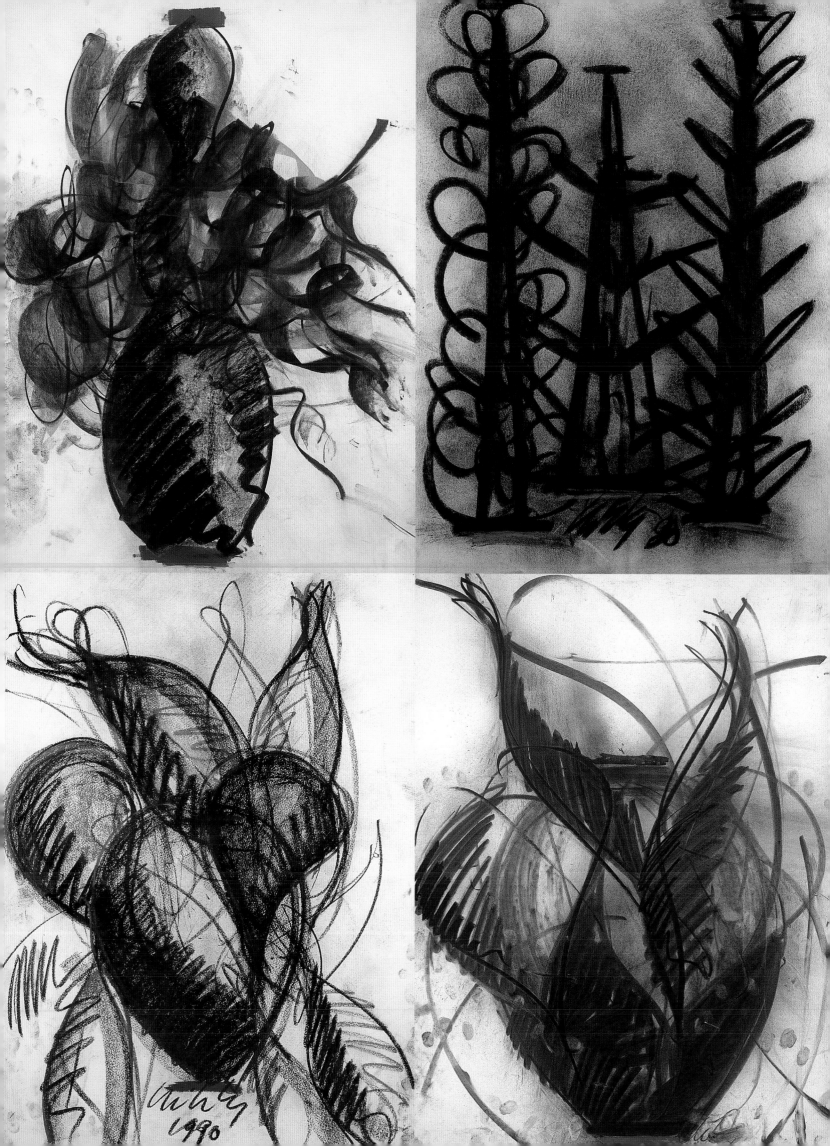

outside inside or both

Rope —
Reel mix

Leaves
Blue mix

River

Plum Putti Ikebana with Single Stem, 1991
27 x 16 x 13"

Cerise Red Piccolo Venetian with Cadmium Red Coils, 1993
9 x 7 x 5"

Gilded Cobalt Piccolo Venetian with Prunts, 2000
11 x 5 x 5"

Naples Yellow Piccolo Venetian with Teal and Sienna Leaves, 1997
16 x 8 x 7"

Milky White Piccolo Venetian with Confetti Speckles, 1997
11 x 5 x 8"

< **Jerusalem 2000 Cylinder,** 1999
14 x 15 x 15"

Jerusalem 2000 Cylinder, 2000
22 x 15 x 10"

Jerusalem 2000 Cylinder, 2000
22 x 18 x 15"

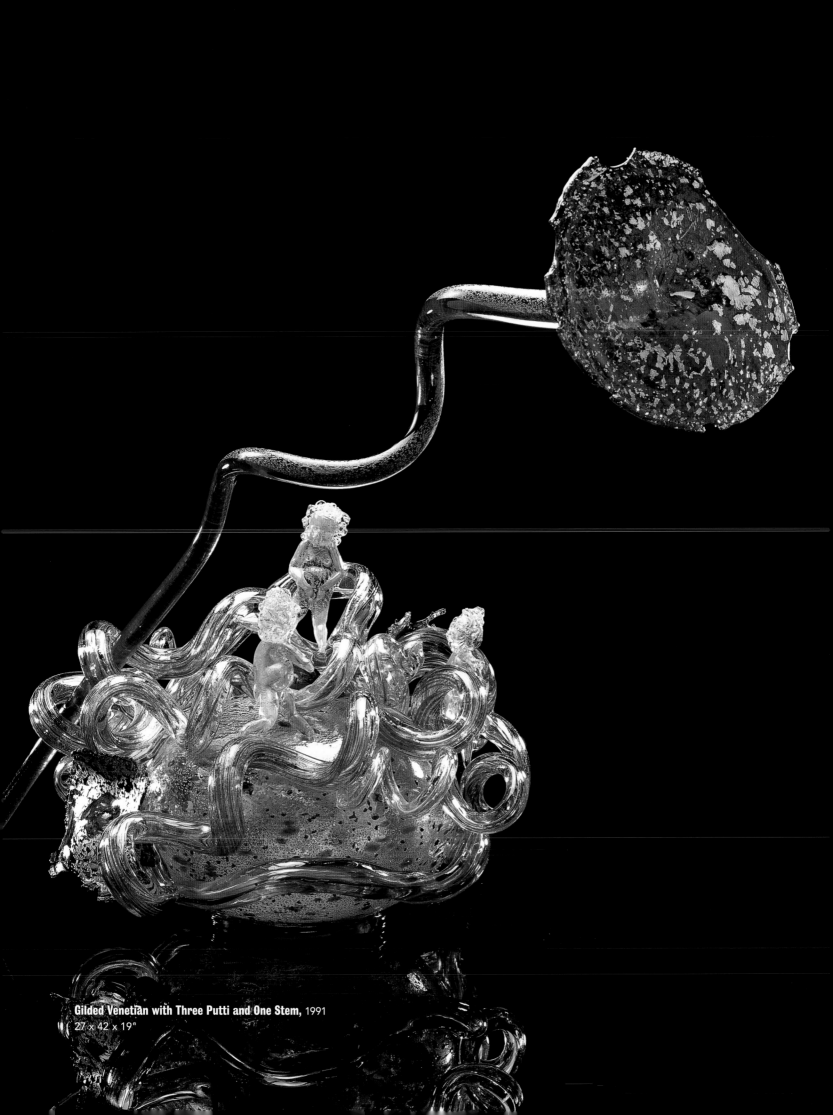

Gilded Venetian with Three Putti and One Stem, 1991
27 x 42 x 19"

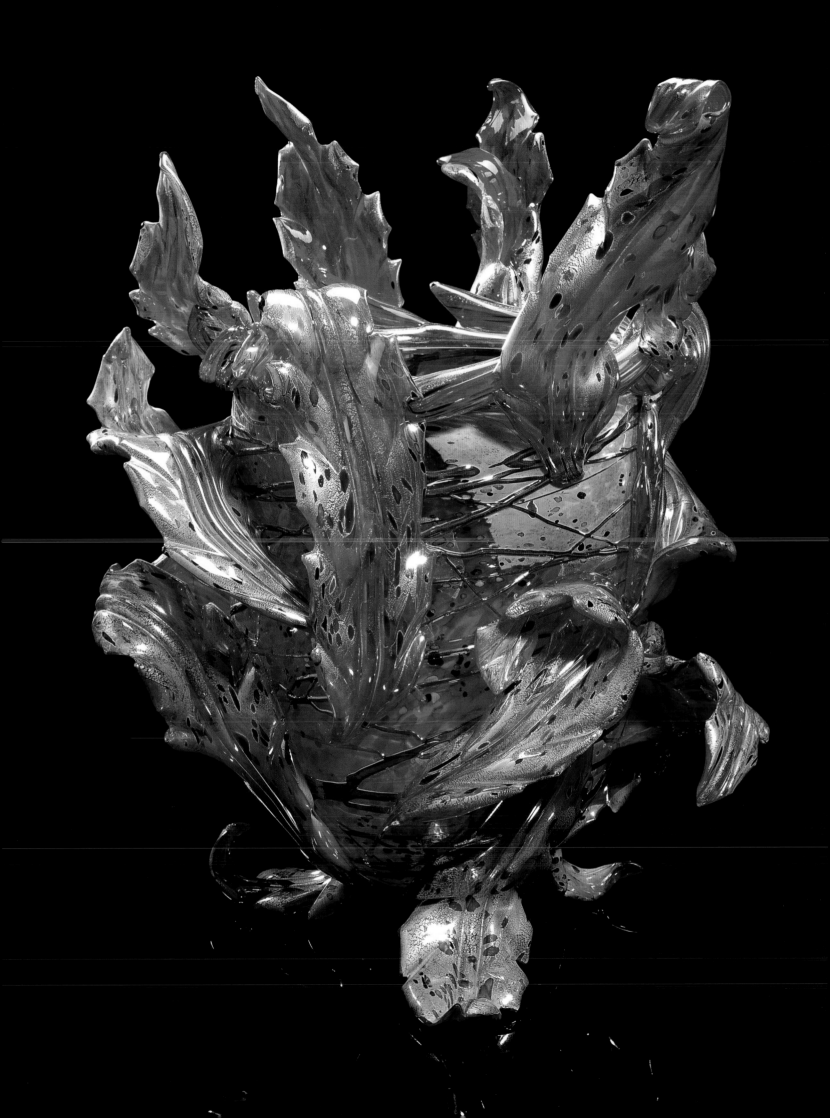

< **Gold over Carmine Venetian with Wrapped Leaves,** 1990
  18 x 14 x 17"

Cerulean Blue Piccolo Venetian, 1998
9 x 5 x 5"

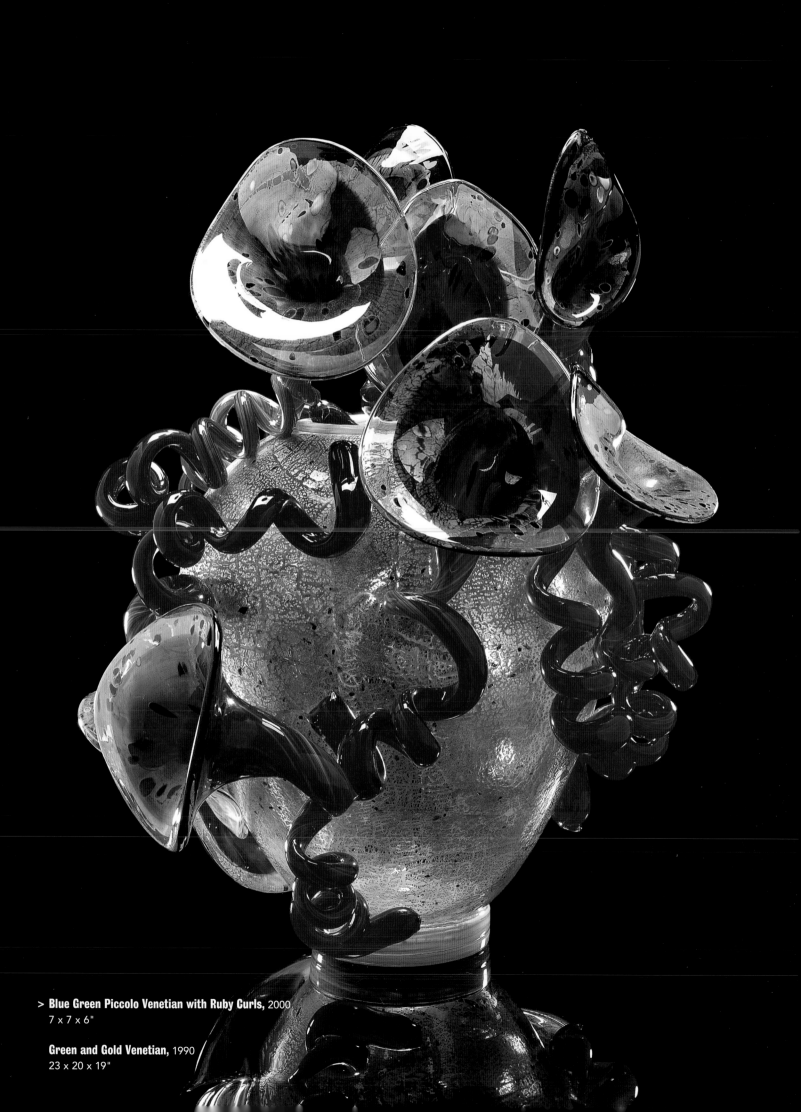

> **Blue Green Piccolo Venetian with Ruby Curls,** 2000
7 x 7 x 6"

Green and Gold Venetian, 1990
23 x 20 x 19"

Jerusalem 2000 Cylinder, 2000
22 x 11 x 14"

< **Oxblood Piccolo Venetian with Raw Sienna Leaves and Coils,** 1994
   4 x 2 x 2"

Terre Verte Venetian, 1990
39 x 14 x 15"

< **Jerusalem 2000 Cylinder,** 1999
34 x 10 x 8"

Jerusalem 2000 Cylinder, 2000
31 x 14 x 12"

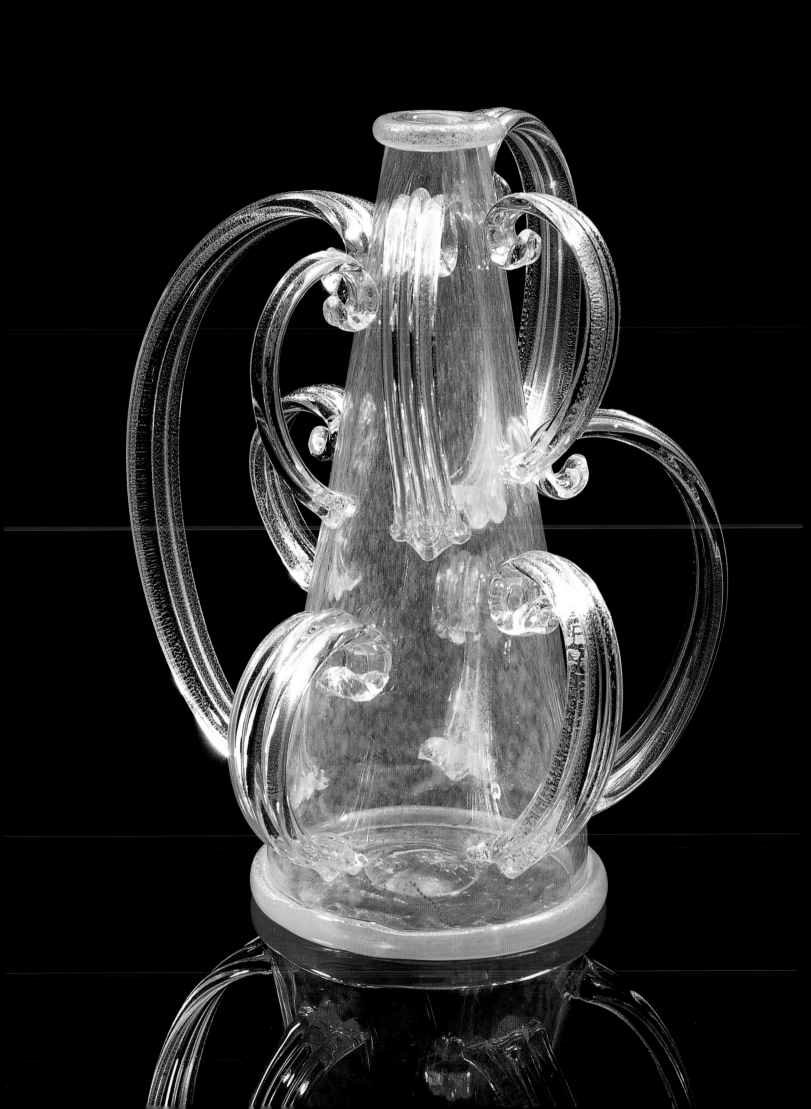

< **Yellow Gold Piccolo Venetian with Handles,** 1998
    10 x 10 x 11"

Golden Piccolo Venetian with Dark Berry Curls, 2000
    12 x 8 x 4"

Gilded Venetian with Burnt Umber Fringe, 1991
15 x 20 x 19"

CHIHULY

AND VENICE

Dan Klein

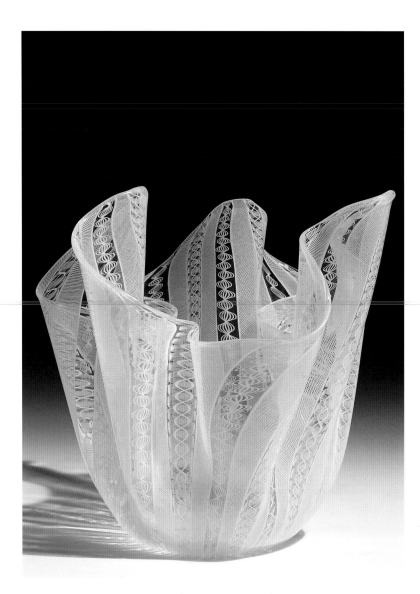

Fazzoletto (handkerchief) vase, 'filigree a reticello' glass, designed by
Fulvio Bianconi and Paolo Venini about 1949, Venini & Co. This example
made 1955. Handkerchief vases were part of Venini production at the
time of Chihuly's visit in 1968. They are still in production today.
Victoria & Albert Museum, inv. Circ270-1955

When Dale Chihuly gets hold of an idea he is unstoppable. He seizes it wholeheartedly, explores it, experiments with it, turns it upside down, expands it beyond any known limits, involves others in the development of his dreams (though they remain his very own), and in the process surprises and delights an audience with something that is completely original. He believes strongly enough in his own vision to make the impossible happen, as he did at Pilchuck Glass School, which he co-founded in 1971 at the age of 29, as he did with the 'Chihuly Over Venice' project twenty-five years later in 1996, as he has done with every new chapter in his life. He has the courage to re-invent himself on a regular basis. His zest for living has had a profound influence on both the masters and the pupils who have been around him. His appetite for learning, particularly about Venetian glass, inspired a whole generation of glassmakers in America at the end of the last century and continues to inspire those new on the scene today.

In 1968, at the age of 26, he made his first prolonged visit to Venice, having been awarded a Louis Comfort Tiffany Foundation Grant for work in glass as well as a Fulbright Fellowship. By this time he had received a B.A. in interior design from the University of Washington in Seattle, an M.S. in sculpture from the University of Wisconsin at Madison studying glassblowing under Harvey Littleton, and an M.F.A. in ceramics from RISD (the Rhode Island School of Design at Providence, Rhode Island). Before going to Venice he had written three hundred letters requesting some sort of internship on Murano. Ludovico de Santillana, the son-in-law of Paolo Venini and the director of the Venini glassworks, was the only one from whom he received a reply. Although he was involved in an architectural project at the factory during his stay there, the main purpose of Chihuly's visit was to understand and absorb the magic of Venetian teamwork and technical wizardry built up over seven hundred years.

Chihuly and other American glassmakers who visited Venice were not able to bring much technique to Venice, 'but they took away inspiration that elevated the whole look of [contemporary] blown studio glass'.[i] In America generally and under Littleton in particular, the emphasis was on the individual. During the 1960s, Americans working in glass sought to explore how feasible it was to express oneself as an artist in this medium. How far could a glass artist go working alone in a studio? Chihuly found a very different ethic in Venice, where 'individual signature styles were shunned in favour of teamwork and intense technical experimentation'.[ii] He returned to the United States having absorbed the 'collaborative master and team approach'.[iii] In 1969 he established a glass program at RISD, where he taught for eleven years, encouraging both individuality and the discipline of teamwork. His students there included a formidable array of names such as Hank Adams, Howard Ben Tré, James Carpenter, Dan Dailey, Michael Glancy, Flora Mace, Mark McDonnell, Benjamin Moore, Pike Powers, Michael Scheiner, Paul Seide, Therman Statom, Steve Weinberg, and Toots Zynsky.

Benjamin Moore, one of Chihuly's students at RISD, had also visited Venice (in 1977), where he had met Lino Tagliapietra, whose brother-in-law had been the first Venetian to teach at Pilchuck, during the previous year. Moore wrote to Chihuly, 'As far as a Venetian glass master for Pilchuck '79, I have another dandy lined up. His name is Lino Tagliapietra. . . . [He] speaks no English, but will be great with the students. . . . [He] is a very unique and rare Venetian glass master'.[iv]

Tagliapietra had always wanted to visit America and was amazed by what he found at Pilchuck. 'I was astounded at the freedom of the students, their lack of hesitation. The boldness was so new to me. On the one hand it was a shock—the lack of cultural base, the absence of traditions. But on the other hand it was very exciting— very inspiring for my own work . . . the lack of restraint in the process, the exciting results'.[v] Norman Courtney, an American glassmaker, commented, 'Lino brought us technique, and everybody realised we had been doing it all wrong'.[vi] Tagliapietra's Venetian virtuosity has had a profound effect on American glass artists generally, and of course on the art of Dale Chihuly. By 1994 the influence of Venice was such that Tagliapietra is quoted as saying, 'I'd say that at least 70% of the technique evidenced in current American glass is absolutely Venetian'.[vii] The fact that Tagliapietra has established a close working relation-ship with America's leading glass artist, in a collaboration that began in 1988 with Chihuly's 'Venetians', is an important contributing factor in this statistic. Chihuly is by no means the only American artist with whom Tagliapietra has collaborated. He has also worked with Dan Dailey, Dorothy Hafner, Marvin Lipofsky, and others.

Chihuly only began working with Tagliapietra after the summer session of Pilchuck in 1987, in a rather casual way and more or less as an experiment. Before that, Chihuly had felt that his own looser and freer style of glassmaking 'had nothing in common with the technically intensive Venetian one'.[viii] In fact, when they started working together more seriously in 1988, working with Tagliapietra on the 'Venetians' freed Chihuly. Implicit faith in Tagliapietra's technical skills allows Chihuly to concentrate on the gestural charcoal, ink, pencil, and watercolour drawings which pour so naturally from him. The drawings are done to music blaring in the background: they are a feast of colour, a reaction to the excitement of the glass-making activities all around him, the outpourings of an imagination bursting with ideas that spill over onto the drawing paper. Chihuly trusts and admires Tagliapietra. They inspire each other. Tagliapietra, used to interpreting

Dale Chihuly (left) working with Lino Tagliapietra (right) at
The Boathouse, 1990

Chartreuse Venetian with One Coil, 1991, 35 x 15 x 15"

the ideas of others, interprets the drawings perfectly. One of Chihuly's great talents is to be able to recognise talent in others, and he is generous as a team leader when using that talent. He allows the virtuosity of his collaborators to assume importance, and the unexpected happens.

The idea of doing a series called 'Venetians' came to Chihuly during a visit to a private apartment in Venice in 1987, when he had seen a collection of 1920s Venetian glass by Martinuzzi, Archimede Seguso, and Artisti Barovier. Much of the vernacular of these Venetians is quoted in the mad multiple handles, the acanthus leaves, and the swirling and twisted add-ons found in Chihuly's 'Venetians'. In typical Chihuly manner, ideas are taken and exaggerated out of all proportion, resulting in a riot of colour and extravagant surface decoration all his own. The 'Venetians' have been described as 'ill-behaved, irritating and threatening',[ix] and yet at the centre of these works, uncharacteristically for Chihuly, is a perfectly formed symmetrical vessel. Chihuly takes a certain pleasure in being irreverent and a bit shocking, but only up to a certain point. 'I do like my things kind of to be universally accepted and not only for a small audience'.[x] He likes to challenge his audience with new ideas, does not allow them to get comfortable with what they have become used to: 'When I begin something new, people usually don't like it. But at the same time when I go into the series for years, they begin to understand it. You have to see something for a while. What looks ugly right now might not look so ugly after a couple of years'.[xi] The 'Venetians' took some getting used to.

Chihuly's collaboration with Tagliapietra was of course not his first encounter with Venetian glass. Venetian glass has with him been a lifelong passion, and as a hot glass artist his way of making glass even in the earliest days of his career must always be associated with Venetian glass history. The aim of the early American pioneers was to work on their own in glass in an atmosphere as far removed as possible from the factory floor. But hot glass requires teamwork, and from the very beginning Chihuly realised this. The more he learnt about Venetian teamwork, the more he visited Venice, and the better he got to know Venetian glassmakers, the more Venetian techniques were used in his way of working. This in turn had an effect on all who were around him either as students or as associates.

Chihuly also worked with two young American 'maestri', Benjamin Moore and Richard Royal, on the 'Venetians'. Moore had already been seduced by the Venetian way of glassmaking on his trips to Murano. Both he and Richard Royal, as well as the virtuoso glassblower William Morris, learnt and taught at Pilchuck and, with Chihuly, Tagliapietra, and others, are responsible for turning Seattle into what has become known as the 'Venice of the West'. With each new gaffer or 'maestro', there are changes of detail in the pieces. Chihuly always remains the master of ceremonies, standing at his table with drawing paper and painting materials, the pro-active side of him drawing and designing pieces, the re-active side alive to what is going on around him, to the creative possibilities that a member of the team might bring to the game. A gesture or a chance happening will suddenly inspire him, and he goes back to the drawing board to capture it. 'Drawing is a fluid process like glassblowing is a fluid process',[xii] Chihuly says. He has always been a talent spotter and uses the talents of others as a springboard for his ideas. In so doing he enriches both his own work and the creative energies of those who work with him. Today Tagliapietra is a world-famous artist in his own right, but his work with Chihuly greatly widened his horizons, unlocking potential that he might otherwise never have discovered in himself.

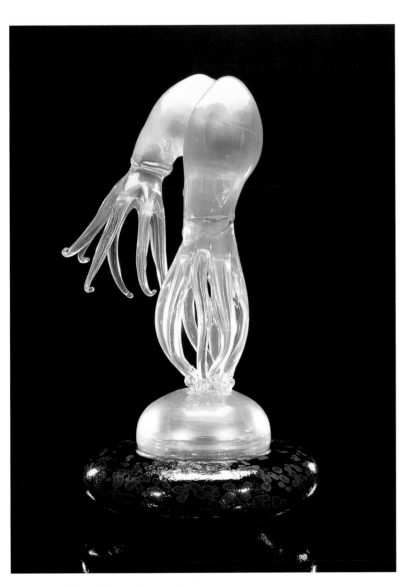

Two Golden Entangled Squid, 1998, 29 x 14 x 13"

Dale Chihuly (center) working with Pino Signoretto (left) at
The Boathouse, 1998

It has been very much the same pattern with Pino Signoretto, the other great Italian 'maestro' to work with Dale Chihuly. In 1992, Signoretto was teaching a class at Pilchuck and asked Chihuly to make a drawing for him to execute in glass. 'I made a drawing of a piece of glass with several cupids on it. Normally I don't like the look of figures in glass, but the putti look just right in glass', Chihuly said. Putti are more commonly depicted in paintings or in wood or plaster sculpture, but in 1999 Chihuly commented, 'The Putto is happier in glass'.[xiii] Over the years the collaboration between Signoretto and Chihuly has developed. A first series of 'Venetians' with Signoretto used the Italian 'maestro's' talents for sculpting in hot glass to add figurative elements to the series. Signoretto spoke little English, as did Tagliapietra in the beginning. The main language of communication in the glass community is body language and the language of glass choreography. In the frenetic processes of handling hot glass, there is little time for language anyway. A thumbs up or an expressive gesture of some sort is the best way of communicating.

In 1999, Chihuly, Signoretto, and their team created another body of work, and a fascinating video has been produced that captures what is required to make the complicated vessels that stand five feet high, with stoppers combining putti and animals. On Murano, Signoretto has his own small factory, where he works with a team of four. Chihuly has made such demands on his extraordinary skills that in a Chihuly session both the pieces and the team have grown to massive proportions. The team grew to fourteen (and on occasion as many as seventeen) people. Once again Chihuly has expanded both his own and Signoretto's artistic and technical limits. With his usual generosity Chihuly says that Signoretto is 'the greatest glass sculptor of our time'.[xiv] The putti and animals combined are, apart from anything, extraordinary feats

Rio Delle Torreselle; 'Chihuly Over Venice',
Venezia Aperto Vetro, 1996

of technical virtuosity. Sculpting a figure in hot glass with expressive gestural details (let alone curly hair) is complicated enough, but to have a putto sitting on a rabbit or kneeling on a fish entails making two complicated figures and joining them together in a feat that demands engineering skills. Only Chihuly would dare to make such demands from the world's most famous sculptor in glass; only Chihuly had the vision to know that the idea was do-able. Chihuly makes light of the brilliance of it all with a characteristic Chihuly sentiment: 'Once I give him the concept, I let him run. . . . Nobody knows better than "The Master"'.[xv]

'Chihuly Over Venice' was equally visionary. The plan was to make a series of chandeliers in glass factories around the world. They were produced at Hackman Nuutajärvi in Finland, at Waterford Crystal in Ireland, at the Vitrocrisa factory in Monterrey, Mexico, at The Boathouse in Seattle, and at Vetreria Signoretto on Murano. In a sort of grand finale, the chandeliers were to be brought together and suspended over the canals of Venice. It was only by chance that in 1996, at very short notice, a glass biennial was planned with the blessing of the Venetian authorities. Chihuly seized the chance of making the 'Chihuly Over Venice' project an important part of the biennial. Against all the odds, permission was granted (sometimes at the eleventh hour) to hang fragile glass sculptures in or near famous Venetian landmarks.

The chandeliers are brilliant structures, composed of simple blown elements, each tied with wire to a central metal armature. Once assembled, the elements hang in a cluster like a gigantic bunch of grapes. They are not chandeliers in the true sense, as most are not self-lighting. They are hanging sculptures. In Venice local by-laws prevented them from being hung. Instead they were suspended within custom-built metal tripod-like supports.

Chandelier in the Palazzo Ducale; 'Chihuly Over Venice',
Venezia Aperto Vetro, 1996

The clear glass chandelier in the Palazzo Ducale was one of the most successful of them. It rose up from the floor like a giant climbing plant that reached upwards to a traditional Murano glass chandelier that hung directly above it, creating a lively dialogue between past and present. The effect was magical. The other chandeliers were monochromatic jewel-like clusters in brilliant colours. As always, the Chihuly colour palette is a thrilling one. Reminiscent of the transformation process in Christo's wrapped buildings and bridges, 'Chihuly Over Venice' cast 'La Serenissma' literally in a new light.

'Chihuly Over Venice' was a festival thought up by an entrepreneur. For Chihuly the glass structures were only a part of the whole. The act of making the work in glass at locations all over the world and assembling the body of work in Venice was a symbolic gesture, a recognition of his debt to Venetian glassmakers, a 'thank you' to Venice. The whole undertaking was more like a Hollywood studio production than a glass exhibition. Filming the story was an important part of the whole. Both the works and the way they are made lend themselves to cinematic treatment. The grand finale in Venice was also used as a grand occasion for celebration and for the most wonderful parties. It is all a part of the Chihuly experience and what has made him such a popular artist.

Artistically speaking, the chandeliers as a whole have added enormously to Chihuly's 'oeuvre'. In conceiving them and making them, he brings together his many talents as a colourist, innovator, and conceptual thinker. The structure devised for making the chandeliers allows Chihuly a great deal of artistic freedom and suits his gestural and instinctive way of working. Creation happens in the process of making. One form suggests the next, allowing his creative juices to flow even as a chandelier is being made. The structural solution also allows Chihuly to think big. He can add almost as many parts as he wishes in this way of working. The chandeliers are not simply random clusters of their individual parts. Their final shape grows organically, so that they take on wholeness in their finished state. One almost forgets that they are made of individual parts in looking up at the single blaze of colour and light that emanates from them.

The book 'Chihuly Over Venice' is dedicated to Ludovico de Santillana, 'an extraordinary man, who took me into his factory when I was a student and allowed me to work and watch the great masters of Venini, an experience that changed my life'.[xvi]

[i] 'Neues Glas' Feb. 1990, p. 88
[ii] 'Dale Chihuly Installations, 1964–1992', Seattle Art Museum, p. 29
[iii] Ibid.
[iv] 'Pilchuck: A Glass School', p. 160
[v] 'Glass' No. 39, 1990, p. 13
[vi] 'Pilchuck: A Glass School', p. 163
[vii] 'Glass' No. 56, Summer 1994, p. 39
[viii] 'Vetro' April/June 2000, p. 15
[ix] 'Glass' No. 39, 1990, p. 22
[x] 'Neues Glas' pp. 17/18
[xi] Ibid.
[xii] 'Chihuly', second edition, revised and expanded, p. 154
[xiii] Quote from video 'Chihuly Working with Pino Signoretto'
[xiv] Ibid.
[xv] Ibid.
[xvi] 'Chihuly Over Venice', 1996, dedication

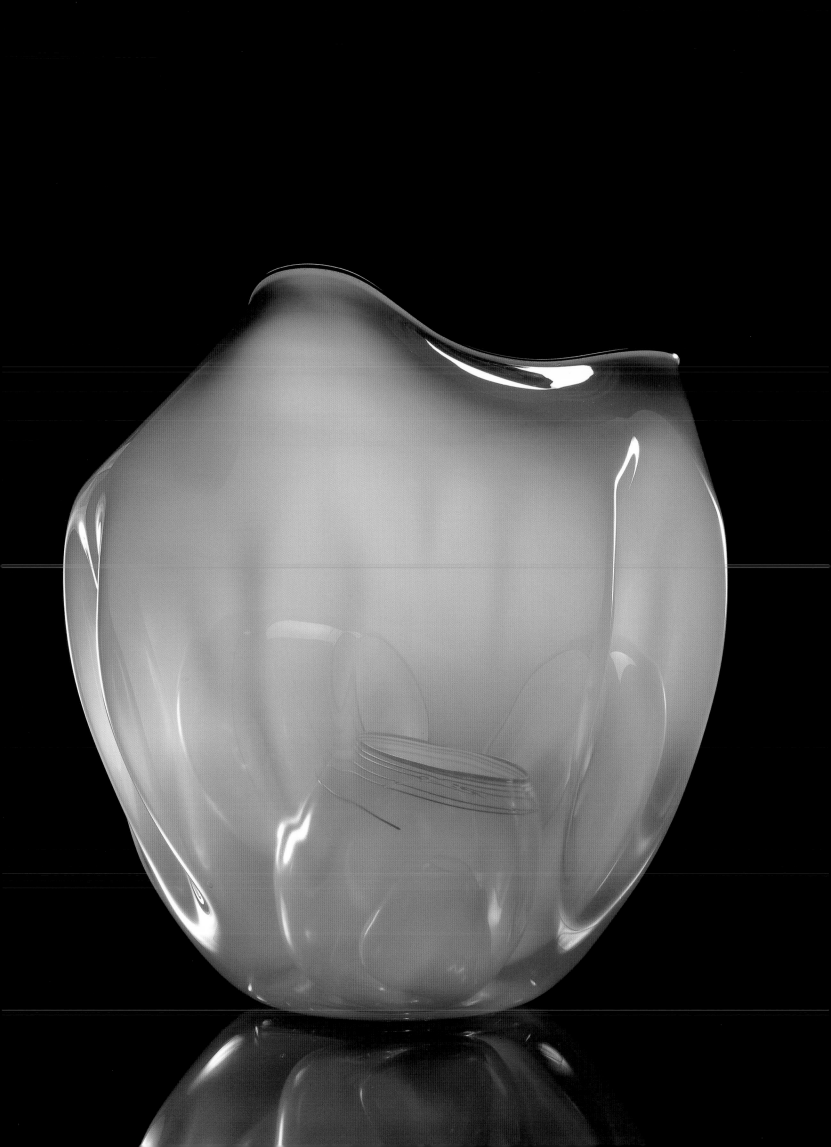

< **Secret Garden Green Basket Set with Black Lip Wraps,** 2000
　17 x 16 x 16"

Early Tabac Basket Set, 1977

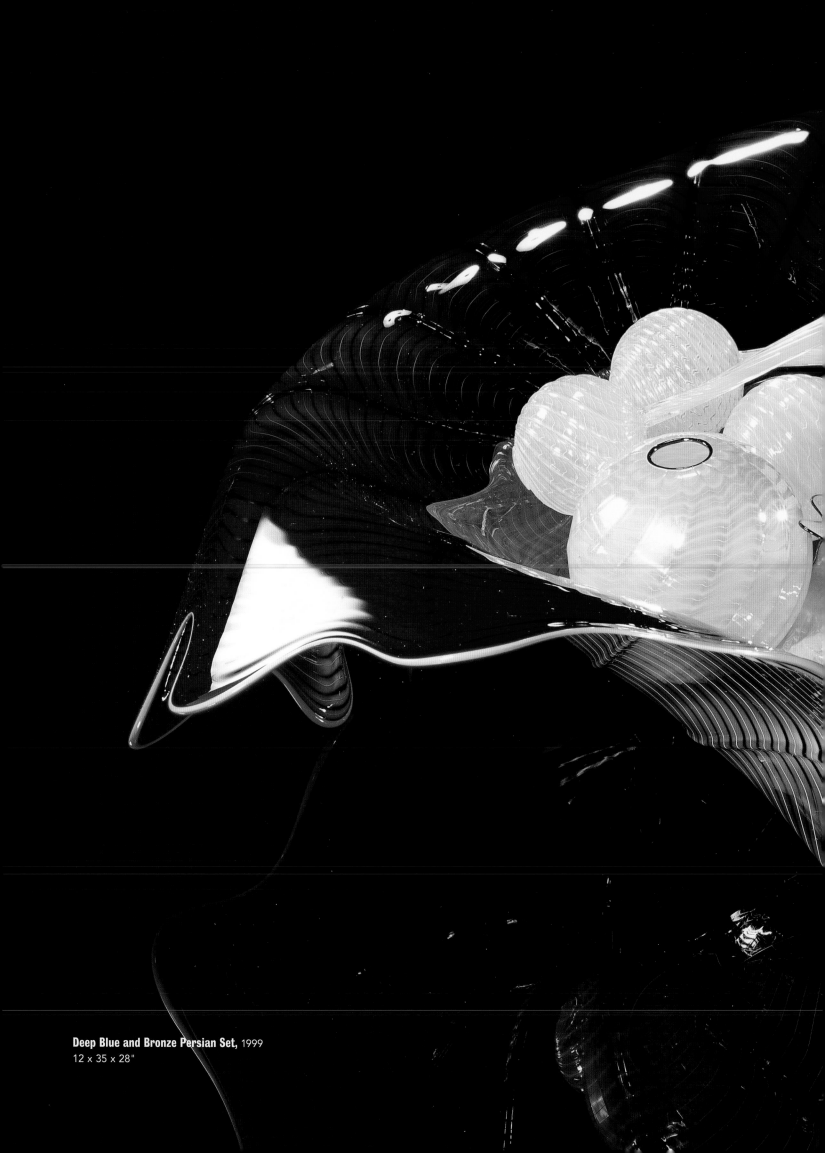

Deep Blue and Bronze Persian Set, 1999
12 x 35 x 28"

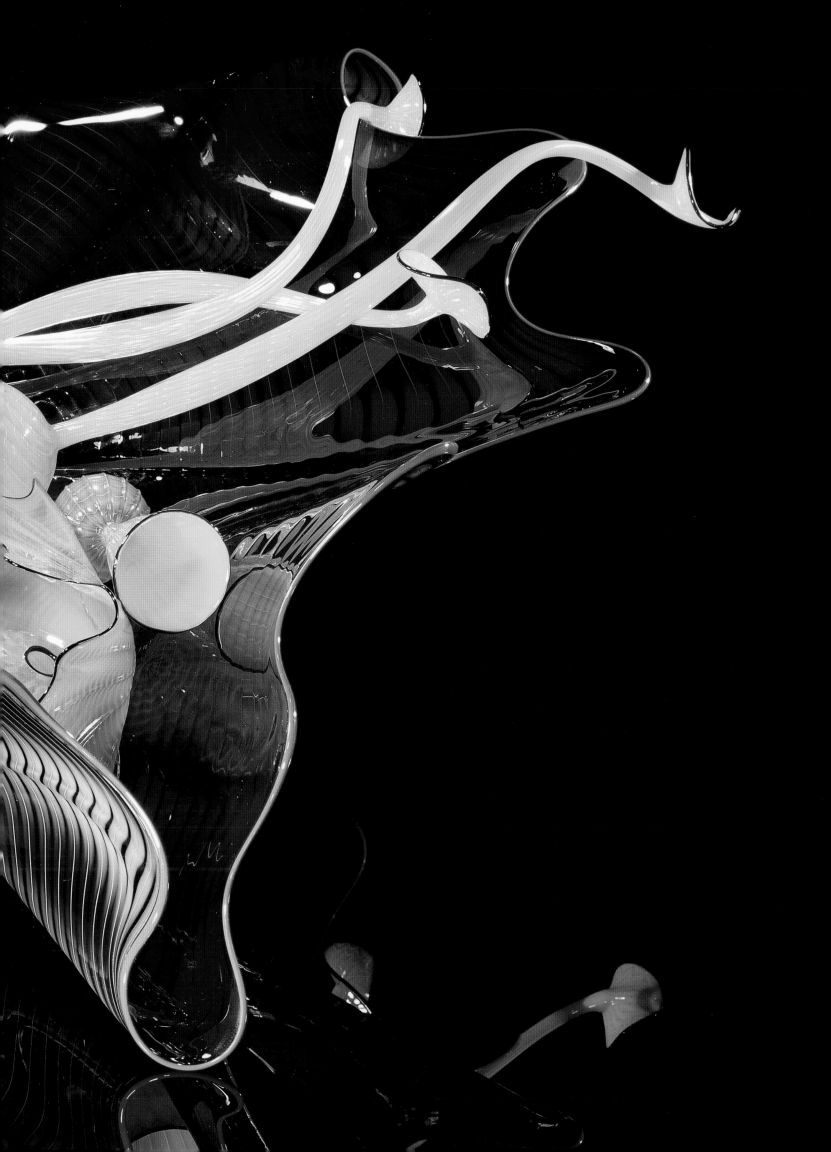

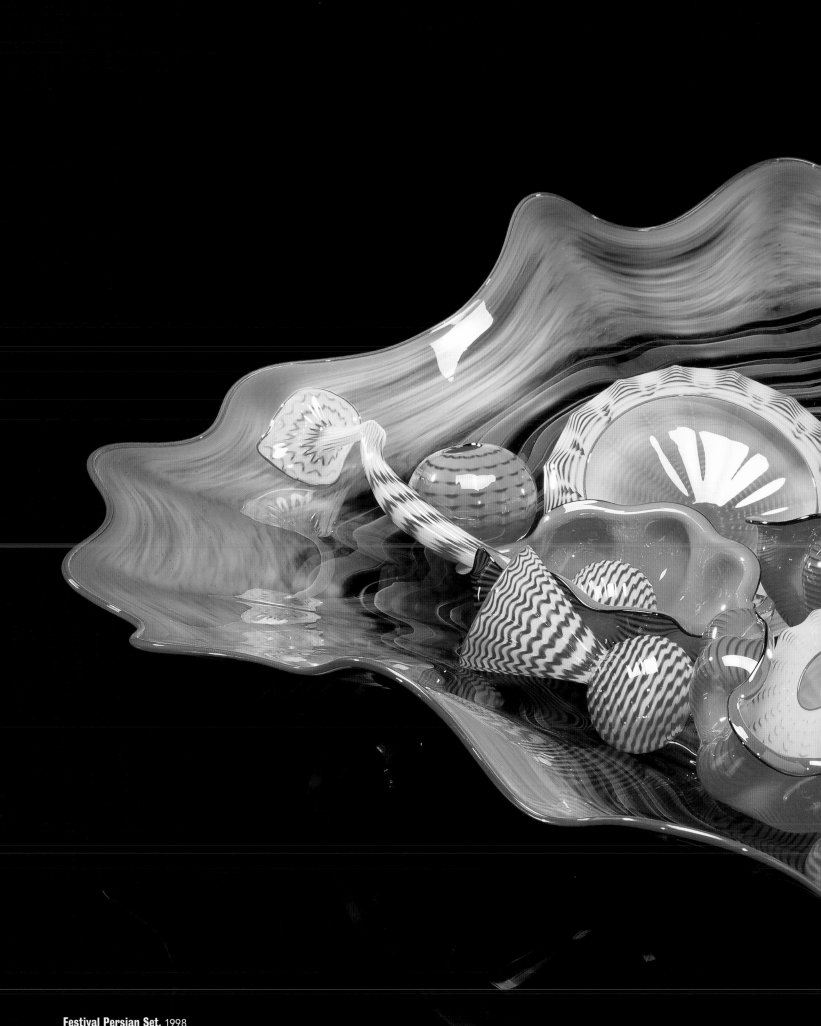

Festival Persian Set, 1998
9 x 42 x 39"

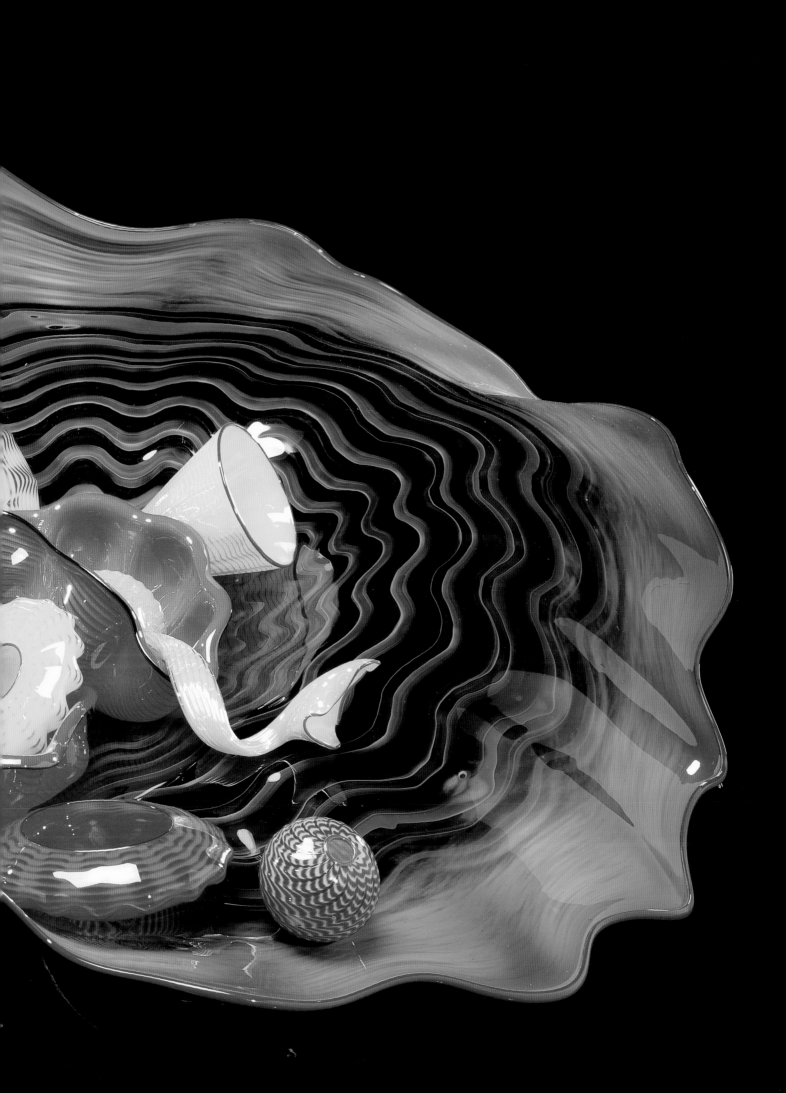

Persian Ceiling, 2000

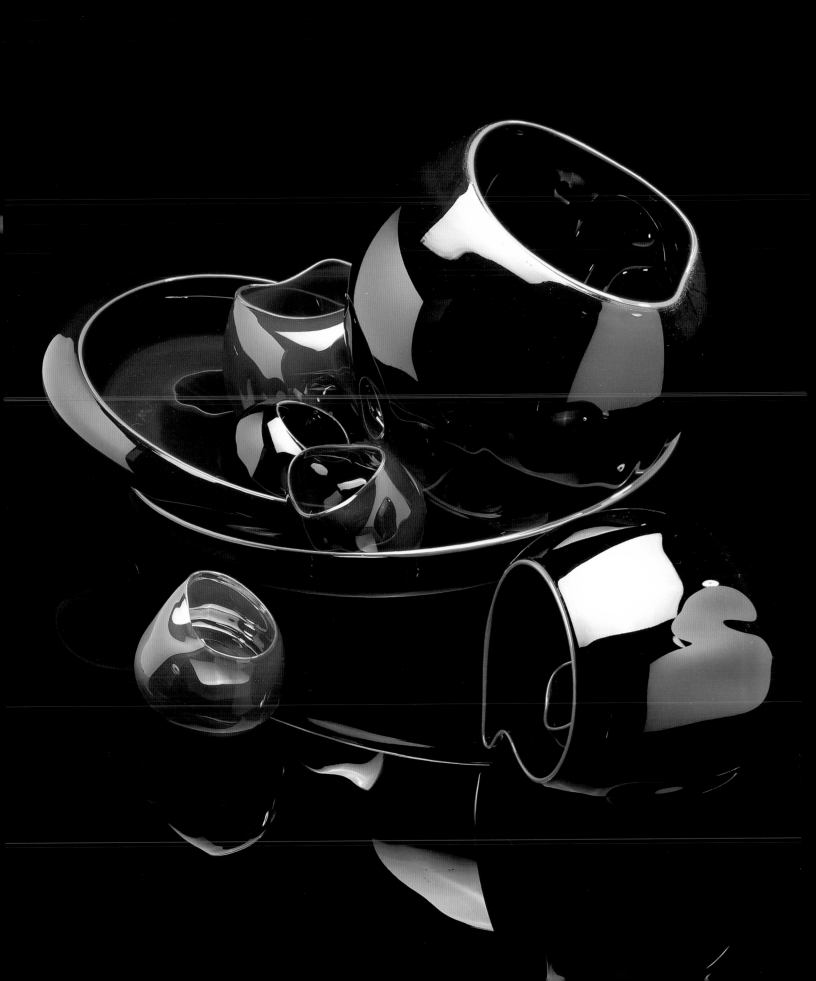

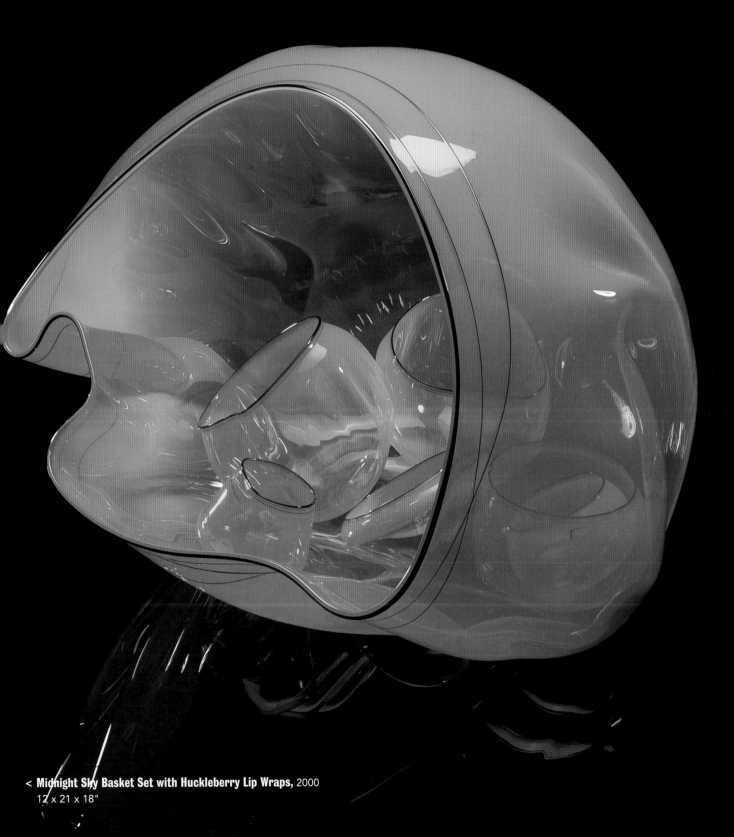

< **Midnight Sky Basket Set with Huckleberry Lip Wraps,** 2000
12 x 21 x 18"

Orpiment Orange Basket Set with Slate Black Lip Wraps, 2001
21 x 20 x 23"

< **Autumn Gold Macchia with Orange Lip Wrap,** 2000
24 x 33 x 30"

Lime Yellow Macchia with Scarlet Lip Wrap, 2000
29 x 42 x 38"

Orange Basket Forest, 2001

Macchia Forest, 2001

CHRONOLOGY

1941 Born September 20 in Tacoma, Washington, to George Chihuly and Viola Magnuson Chihuly. George Chihuly is a butcher by trade and a union organizer. Viola Chihuly is a homemaker and avid gardener. The family's ancestry is predominantly Hungarian, Czech, and Slavic on the Chihuly side and Swedish and Norwegian on the Magnuson side.

1957 Older brother and only sibling, George, is killed in a Navy Air Force training accident in Pensacola, Florida.

1958 His father suffers a fatal heart attack at age 51. His mother goes to work to support herself and Dale.

1959 Graduates from high school in Tacoma. Although he has no interest in pursuing a formal education, his mother persuades him to enroll in the College of Puget Sound (now the University of Puget Sound) in his hometown. Two accomplishments the following year—a term paper on Van Gogh and the remodeling of the recreation room in his mother's home—motivate him to transfer to the University of Washington in Seattle to study interior design and architecture.

1961 Joins Delta Kappa Epsilon fraternity and becomes rush chairman. Learns to melt and fuse glass.

1962 Disillusioned with his studies, he drops out of school and travels to Florence to study art. Discouraged by not being able to speak Italian, he leaves and travels to the Middle East.

1963 Works on a kibbutz in the Negev Desert. Meets architect Robert Landsman in Jericho, Jordan, and they visit the site of ancient Petra together. Redirected after meeting Landsman and spending a year abroad, he returns to the University of Washington in the College of Arts and Sciences and studies under Hope Foote and Warren Hill. In a weaving class with Doris Brockway, he incorporates glass shards into woven tapestries.

1964 While still a student, receives the Seattle Weavers Guild Award for his innovative use of glass and fiber. Returns to Europe, visits Leningrad, and makes the first of many trips to Ireland.

1965 Receives B.A. in Interior Design from the University of Washington and works as a designer for John Graham Architects in Seattle. Introduced to textile designer Jack Lenor Larsen, who becomes a mentor and friend.

Experimenting on his own in his basement studio, Chihuly blows his first glass bubble by melting stained glass and using a metal pipe. Awarded Highest Honors from the American Institute of Interior Designers (now ASID).

1966 Works as a commercial fisherman in Alaska to earn money for graduate school. Enters the University of Wisconsin at Madison, on a full scholarship, where he studies glassblowing under Harvey Littleton. It was the first glass program in the United States.

1967 Receives M.S. in Sculpture from the University of Wisconsin. Enrolls at the Rhode Island School of Design (RISD) in Providence, where he begins his exploration of environmental works using neon, argon, and blown glass. Visits the Montreal World Exposition '67 and is inspired by the architectural glass works of Stanislav Libenský and Jaroslava Brychtová at the Czechoslovak pavilion. Awarded a Louis Comfort Tiffany Foundation Grant for work in glass. Italo Scanga, then on the faculty at Pennsylvania State University's Art Department, lectures at RISD, and the two begin a lifelong friendship. They consider themselves brothers.

1968 Receives M.F.A. in Ceramics from RISD. Awarded a Fulbright Fellowship, which enables him to travel and work in Europe. Invited by architect Ludovico de Santillana, son-in-law of Paolo Venini, Chihuly becomes the first American glassblower to work in the prestigious Venini factory on the island of Murano. Returns to the United States and spends the first of four consecutive summers teaching at Haystack Mountain School of Crafts in Deer Isle, Maine. There he meets Director Fran Merritt, who becomes a friend and lifetime mentor. Visits "The Block" (Block Island) for the first time, his favorite retreat in the United States.

1969 Travels again, this time with his mother, throughout Europe, visiting relatives in Sweden and making pilgrimages to meet glass masters Erwin Eisch in Germany and Jaroslava Brychtová and Stanislav Libenský in Czechoslovakia. Returning to the United States, Chihuly establishes the glass program at RISD, where he teaches for the next fifteen years. Students include James Carpenter, Dan Dailey, Toots Zynsky, Roni Horn, Howard Ben Tré, Michael Glancy, Pike Powers, Hank Adams, Therman Statom, Paul Seide, Steve Weinberg, Michael Scheiner, Benjamin Moore, Flora Mace, and Mark McDonnell.

1970 Chihuly and friends shut down RISD in protests over the Cambodian offensive. During the strike, Chihuly and student John Landon develop ideas for an alternative school in the Pacific Northwest, inspired by Haystack Mountain School of Crafts. Meets artist Buster Simpson, who later works with Chihuly and Landon at the school. Meets James Carpenter, a student in the illustration department, and they begin a four-year collaboration.

1971 On the site of a tree farm donated by Seattle art patrons Anne Gould Hauberg and John Hauberg, the Pilchuck Glass School is created. A $2,000 grant to Chihuly and Ruth Tamura from the Union of Independent Colleges of Art and additional funding from the Haubergs provide seed money for this innovative new school. From this modest beginning, Pilchuck Glass School becomes an institution that will have a profound impact on artists working in glass worldwide. Chihuly's first environmental installation at Pilchuck is created that summer. In the fall he resumes teaching at RISD and creates "20,000 Pounds of Ice and Neon" and "Glass Forest #1," and "Glass Forest #2" with James Carpenter, installations that prefigure later environmental works by Chihuly.

1972 While he is at Pilchuck, his studio on Hobart Street in Providence burns down. Returns to Venice with Carpenter to blow glass for the "Glas heute" exhibition at the Museum Bellerive, Zurich, Switzerland. He and Carpenter continue to collaborate on large-scale architectural projects, and, confining themselves to the use of static architectural structures, they create "Rondel Door" and "Cast Glass Door" at Pilchuck. Back in Providence, they create "Dry Ice, Bent Glass and Neon," a conceptual breakthrough.

1974 Returns to Europe, this time on a tour of European glass centers with Thomas Buechner of the Corning Museum of Glass and Paul Schulze, head of the Design Department at Steuben Glass. Makes his first significant purchase of art, "La Donna Perfecta," an art-deco glass mosaic. Upon returning to the United States, he builds a glass shop for the Institute of American Indian Arts in Santa Fe, New Mexico. Supported by a National Endowment for the Arts grant at Pilchuck, James Carpenter, a group of students, and he develop a technique for picking up glass thread drawings. In December at RISD, he completes his last collaborative project with Carpenter, "Corning Wall."

1975 At RISD, begins series of "Navajo Blanket Cylinders." Kate Elliott and, later, Flora Mace

fabricate the complex thread drawings. He receives the first of two National Endowment for the Arts Individual Artist grants. Artist-in-residence with Seaver Leslie at Artpark, on the Niagara Gorge, in New York State. Begins "Irish" and "Ulysses" cylinders with Leslie and Mace.

1976 Travels with Seaver Leslie to the British Isles and Ireland. An automobile accident in England leaves him, after weeks in the hospital and 256 stitches in his face, without sight in his left eye and with permanent damage to his right ankle and foot. After recuperating at the home of painter Peter Blake, he returns to Providence to serve as head of the Department of Sculpture and the Program in Glass at RISD. He invites Robert Grosvenor, Fairfield Porter, Dennis Oppenheim, Alan Seret, and John Torreano to RISD as visiting artists. Henry Geldzahler, curator of contemporary art at the Metropolitan Museum of Art in New York, acquires three "Navajo Blanket Cylinders" for the museum's collection. This is a turning point in Chihuly's career, and a friendship between artist and curator commences.

1977 Inspired by Northwest Coast Indian baskets he sees at the Washington Historical Society in Tacoma, begins the "Basket" series at Pilchuck over the summer, with Benjamin Moore as his assistant gaffer. Continues his bicoastal teaching assignments, dividing his time between Rhode Island and the Pacific Northwest. Charles Cowles curates a three-person show of the work of Chihuly, Italo Scanga, and James Carpenter at the Seattle Art Museum.

1978 Meets William Morris, a student at Pilchuck Glass School, and the two begin a close, eight-year working relationship. A solo show curated by Michael W. Monroe at the Renwick Gallery, Smithsonian Institution, in Washington, D.C., is another milestone in Chihuly's career.

1979 Dislocates his shoulder in a bodysurfing accident and relinquishes the gaffer position for good. William Morris becomes his chief gaffer for the next several years. Chihuly begins to make drawings as a way to communicate his designs. Together with Morris, Benjamin Moore, and student assistants Michael Scheiner and Rich Royal, he blows glass in Baden, Austria.

1980 Resigns his teaching position at RISD. He returns there periodically during the 1980s as artist-in-residence. Begins "Seaform Series" at Pilchuck in the summer and later, back in Providence, returns to architectural installations with the creation of windows for the Shaare Emeth Synagogue in St. Louis, Missouri.

Purchases his first building, the Boathouse, in Pawtuxet Cove, Rhode Island, for his residence and studio.

1981 Begins "Macchia" series, using up to three hundred colors of glass. These wildly spotted, brightly colored forms are dubbed "the uglies" by his mother, but they are eventually christened "Macchia," Italian for "spotted," by his friend Italo Scanga.

1982 With William Morris, tours one thousand miles of Brittany by bicycle in the spring. First major catalog is published: "Chihuly Glass," designed by an RISD colleague and friend, Malcolm Grear.

1983 Sells the Boathouse in Rhode Island and returns to the Pacific Northwest after sixteen years on the East Coast. Works at Pilchuck in the fall and winter, further developing the "Macchia" series with William Morris as chief gaffer.

1984 Returning to the cylinder form, at RISD and Carnegie-Mellon in Pittsburgh, begins work on the "Soft Cylinder" series with Flora Mace and Joey Kirkpatrick executing the glass drawings. He is honored as RISD President's Fellow at the Whitney Museum in New York and receives the Visual Artists Award from the American Council for the Arts, as well as the first of three state Governor's Arts Awards.

1985 Begins working hot glass on a larger scale and creates several site-specific installations, including "Puget Sound Forms" for the Seattle Aquarium. Experiments with "Flower Forms." Returns to Baden, Austria, this time to teach with William Morris, Flora Mace, and Joey Kirkpatrick. Travels to Malta and the Channel Islands. Purchases the Buffalo Shoe Company building on the east side of Lake Union in Seattle and begins restoring it for use as a primary studio and residence.

1986 Begins "Persian" series with Martin Blank, a former RISD student and assistant, as gaffer. With the opening of "Objets de Verre" at the Musée des Arts Décoratifs, Palais du Louvre, in Paris, he becomes one of only four American artists to have had a one-person exhibition at the Louvre. Receives honorary doctorates from both the University of Puget Sound, Tacoma, and RISD, Providence.

1987 Establishes his first hotshop in the Van de Kamp building near Lake Union. Donates permanent retrospective collection to the Tacoma Art Museum in memory of his brother and father. Begins association with artist Parks Anderson, commencing with the "Rainbow Room Frieze," a permanent installation for the Rainbow Room at Rockefeller Center in New York City. Marries playwright Sylvia Peto.

1988 Inspired by a private collection of Italian art-deco glass, primarily designed by Martinuzzi and Scarpa, Chihuly begins "Venetian"series. Working from Chihuly's drawings, Lino Tagliapietra serves as gaffer. Receives an honorary doctorate from the California College of Arts and Crafts, Oakland.

1989 With Italian glass masters Lino Tagliapietra, Pino Signoretto, and a team of glassblowers at Pilchuck Glass School, begins "Putti Venetian" series. Working with Tagliapietra, Chihuly creates "Ikebana" series, inspired by his travels to Japan and exposure to ikebana masters.

1990 Purchases the historic Pocock Building located on Lake Union, realizing his dream of being on the water in Seattle. Renovates the building and names it The Boathouse, for use as a studio, hotshop, archives, and residence. Travels to Japan.

1991 Begins "Niijima Float" series with Rich Royal as gaffer, creating some of the largest pieces of glass ever blown by hand. Completes a number of large-scale architectural installations, including those for GTE World Headquarters in Irving, Texas, and the Yasui Konpira-gu Shinto Shrine in Kyoto, Japan. He and Sylvia Peto divorce.

1992 Begins "Chandelier" series with a large-scale hanging sculpture for the exhibition "Dale Chihuly: Installations 1964–1992," curated by Patterson Sims at the Seattle Art Museum. Honored as the first National Living Treasure by the Institute for Human Potential, University of North Carolina, Wilmington. Designs sets for Seattle Opera production of Debussy's "Pelléas et Mélisande," which premieres in 1993. The "Pilchuck Stumps" are created during this project but are not widely exhibited.

1993 Begins "Piccolo Venetian" series with Lino Tagliapietra. Alumni Association of the University of Washington names him Alumnus Summa Laude Dignatus, its most prestigious honor. Creates "100,000 Pounds of Ice and Neon," a temporary installation in the Tacoma Dome, Tacoma, Washington, attended by 35,000 visitors in four days.

1994 "Chihuly at Union Station," five large-scale installations for Tacoma's Union Station Federal Courthouse, is sponsored by the Executive Council for a Greater Tacoma and organized by the Tacoma Art Museum. Hilltop Artists in Residence, a glassblowing program for at-risk youths in Tacoma, Washington, is created by friend Kathy Kaperick; Chihuly assists with instruction of youths and is a major contributor. The Brooklyn Museum in New York commissions a temporary installation for its Grand Lobby. Discussions begin on a project to build the Museum of Glass on the Thea Foss Waterway in Tacoma and to design "The Chihuly Bridge," which will connect the glass center to Tacoma's university district.

1995 "Cerulean Blue Macchia with Chartreuse Lip Wrap" is added to the White House Collection of American Crafts. "Chihuly Over Venice" begins with a glassblowing session in Nuutajärvi, Finland, and a subsequent blow at the Waterford Crystal factory, Ireland. Creates "Chihuly e Spoleto," an installation for the 38th Spoleto Festival of the Two Worlds, in Spoleto, Italy. Receives an honorary doctorate from Pratt Institute, New York.

1996 "Chihuly Over Venice" continues with a blow in Monterrey, Mexico, and culminates with the installation of fourteen "Chandeliers" at various sites in Venice. The exhibition "Chihuly Over Venice" begins its national tour at the Kemper Museum of Contemporary Art & Design in Kansas City, Missouri. Chihuly purchases the Ballard Building in Seattle for use as mock-up and studio space. Creates a major installation for the Academy of Motion Picture Arts and Sciences Governor's Ball following the Academy Awards ceremony in Hollywood, California. Creates his first permanent outdoor installation, "Icicle Creek Chandelier," for the Sleeping Lady Conference Retreat in Leavenworth, Washington. Receives an honorary doctorate from Gonzaga University, Spokane, Washington.

1997 Continues and expands series of experimental plastics he calls "polyvitro" in his newly renovated Ballard studio. "Chihuly" is designed by Massimo Vignelli and co-published by Harry N. Abrams, Inc., New York, and Portland Press, Seattle. A permanent installation of Chihuly's work opens at the Hakone Glass Forest, Ukai Museum, in Hakone, Japan. Chihuly and his team invite local high school students to photograph a blow and installation at the Vianne factory in France. Viola Chihuly is 90.

1998 Chihuly is invited to Sydney, Australia, with his team to participate in the Sydney Arts Festival. A son, Jackson Viola Chihuly, is born February 12 to Dale Chihuly and Leslie Jackson. Hilltop Artists in Residence program expands to Taos, New Mexico, to work with Taos Pueblo Native Americans. Two large "Chandeliers" are created for Benaroya Hall, the home of the Seattle Symphony. Chihuly's largest sculpture to date, the "Fiori di Como," is installed in the lobby of the Bellagio in Las Vegas. Creates a major permanent installation consisting of the "Temple of the Sun," "Temple of the Moon," "Crystal Gate," and the "Atlantis Chandelier" for Atlantis on Paradise Island, Bahamas. PBS stations across the United States air "Chihuly Over Venice," the nation's first high-definition television (HDTV) broadcast.

1999 Begins "Jerusalem Cylinder" series. In celebration of the millennium, Chihuly mounts his most ambitious exhibition to date: "Chihuly in the Light of Jerusalem 2000," for which he creates seventeen installations within the stone walls of an ancient military fortress, currently known as the Tower of David Museum of the History of Jerusalem. Travels to the Victoria and Albert Museum, London, to unveil an eighteen-foot "Chandelier" gracing the main entrance of the museum. Returns to Jerusalem to create a sixty-foot wall from twenty-four massive blocks of ice shipped from Alaska.

2000 Designs an installation for the White House Millennium Celebration. Creates "La Tour de Lumière" sculpture as part of the exhibition "Contemporary American Sculpture in Monte Carlo." Marlborough Gallery represents Chihuly. More than a million visitors enter the Tower of David Museum to see "Chihuly in the Light of Jerusalem 2000," breaking the world attendance record for a temporary exhibition during 1999–2000. Receives an honorary doctorate from Brandeis University, Waltham, Massachusetts. "Chihuly Projects" is published by Portland Press and distributed by Harry N. Abrams, Inc.

2001 "Chihuly at the V&A" opens in London. Exhibits at Marlborough Gallery, New York and London. Creates a series of intertwining "Chandeliers" for the Gonda Building at the Mayo Clinic in Rochester, Minnesota. Begins major commission for the Universal Oceanographic Park in Valencia, Spain, and exhibits artwork throughout the city.

MUSEUM EXHIBITIONS

1967
Dale Chihuly
University of Wisconsin,
Madison, Wisconsin

1971
Glass Environment: Dale Chihuly &
James Carpenter
American Craft Museum,
New York, New York

1975
Dale Chihuly: Indian Blanket Cylinders
Utah Museum of Fine Arts,
Salt Lake City, Utah
Institute of American Indian Arts Museum,
Santa Fe, New Mexico

1976
Dale Chihuly: Glass Cylinders
Wadsworth Atheneum,
Hartford, Connecticut
Dale Chihuly: Indian Blanket Cylinders
David Winton Bell Gallery, Brown University,
Providence, Rhode Island
Leigh Yawkey Woodson Art Museum,
Wausau, Wisconsin

1978
Baskets and Cylinders: Recent Glass by
Dale Chihuly
Renwick Gallery, National Museum
of American Art, Smithsonian Institution,
Washington, D.C.

1979
Dale Chihuly/VIDRO
Museu de Arte de São Paulo,
São Paulo, Brazil

1980
Dale Chihuly: An American Glass Artist
Eretz Israel Museum,
Tel Aviv, Israel
Dale Chihuly: Recent Works
Fine Arts Center Galleries, University
of Rhode Island,
Kingston, Rhode Island

1981
Dale Chihuly: Glass
Tacoma Art Museum,
Tacoma, Washington

1982
Dale Chihuly: Glass
Phoenix Art Museum,
Phoenix, Arizona

Dale Chihuly: Recent Works in Glass
Tucson Museum of Art,
Tucson, Arizona
San Diego Museum of Art,
San Diego, California

1983
Dale Chihuly: Recent Works in Glass
Saint Louis Art Museum,
St. Louis, Missouri
Palm Springs Desert Museum,
Palm Springs, California

1984
Chihuly: A Decade of Glass
Bellevue Art Museum,
Bellevue, Washington
Modern Art Museum of Fort Worth,
Fort Worth, Texas
Dale Chihuly: Recent Works in Glass
Crocker Art Museum,
Sacramento, California

1985
Chihuly: A Decade of Glass
Arkansas Arts Center,
Little Rock, Arkansas
Madison Art Center,
Madison, Wisconsin
Palmer Museum of Art,
Pennsylvania State University,
University Park, Pennsylvania
University Galleries, Illinois State University,
Normal, Illinois

1986
Chihuly: A Decade of Glass
Brunnier Art Museum, Iowa State University,
Ames, Iowa
Chicago Cultural Center,
Chicago, Illinois
Mint Museum of Art,
Charlotte, North Carolina
Muskegon Museum of Art,
Muskegon, Michigan
Musée des Arts Décoratifs de Montréal,
Montreal, Quebec, Canada
Dale Chihuly: Objets de Verre
Musée des Arts Décoratifs, Palais du Louvre,
Paris, France

1987
Chihuly: A Decade of Glass
Fred Jones Jr. Museum of Art, University
of Oklahoma,
Norman, Oklahoma
Art Museum of Western Virginia,
Roanoke, Virginia
Dale Chihuly: Objets de Verre
Musée Matisse, Le Cateau–Cambrésis, France

1988
Chihuly: Persians
DIA Art Foundation,
Bridgehampton, New York
Dale Chihuly: Objets de Verre
Fundação Calouste Gulbenkian,
Lisbon, Portugal
Musée d'Unterlinden,
Colmar, France

1989
Chihuly: Persians
Society for Contemporary Craft,
Pittsburgh, Pennsylvania
20ª Bienal Internacional de São Paulo
São Paulo, Brazil

1990
Chihuly: Glass Master
Museo Nacional de Bellas Artes,
Santiago, Chile
Dale Chihuly: Japan 1990
Azabu Museum of Arts and Crafts,
Tokyo, Japan
Dale Chihuly: Persians
Hudson River Museum of Westchester,
Yonkers, New York

1991
Chihuly: Venetians
Uměleckoprůmsylové muzeum,
Prague, Czech Republic
Röhsska Konstslöjdmuseet,
Göteborg, Sweden

1992
Chihuly Courtyards
Honolulu Academy of Arts,
Honolulu, Hawaii
Dale Chihuly: Glass
Taipei Fine Arts Museum,
Taipei, Taiwan
Dale Chihuly: Installations
Seattle Art Museum,
Seattle, Washington
Contemporary Arts Center,
Cincinnati, Ohio
Dale Chihuly: Venetians
Museum für Kunst und Gewerbe Hamburg,
Hamburg, Germany
Nationaal Glasmuseum, Leerdam,
The Netherlands
Museum voor modern kunst,
Oostende, Belgium
Dale Chihuly
Toledo Museum of Art,
Toledo, Ohio

1993
Chihuly: alla Macchia
Art Museum of Southeast Texas,
Beaumont, Texas
Chihuly in Australia: Glass and Works on Paper
Powerhouse Museum,
Sydney, Australia
National Gallery of Victoria,
Melbourne, Australia
Scitech Discovery Centre,
Perth, Australia
Chihuly: Form from Fire
Lowe Art Museum, University of Miami,
Coral Gables, Florida
Tampa Museum of Art,
Tampa, Florida
Museum of Arts and Sciences,
Daytona Beach, Florida
Dale Chihuly: Installations
Detroit Institute of Arts,
Detroit, Michigan
Dale Chihuly: Virtuose Spiele in Glas
Altes Zeughaus Landenberg,
Sarnen, Switzerland
Historiches Museum,
Sarnen, Switzerland

1994
Chihuly: alla Macchia
Austin Museum of Art–Laguna Gloria,
Austin, Texas
Chihuly Baskets
North Central Washington Museum,
Wenatchee, Washington
Port Angeles Fine Arts Center,
Port Angeles, Washington
Chihuly: Form from Fire
Philharmonic Center for the Arts,
Naples, Florida
Center for the Arts,
Vero Beach, Florida
Samuel P. Harn Museum of Art,
University of Florida,
Gainesville, Florida
Museum of Fine Arts, Florida State University,
Tallahassee, Florida
Chihuly: Glass in Architecture
Kaohsiung Museum of Fine Arts,
Kaohsiung, Taiwan
Dale Chihuly: Installations
Dallas Museum of Art,
Dallas, Texas
Santa Barbara Museum of Art,
Santa Barbara, California
Chihuly in New Zealand: Glass and Works on Paper
Dowse Art Museum,
Lower Hutt, New Zealand
Waikato Museum of Art and History,
Hamilton, New Zealand

Otago Museum,
Dunedin, New Zealand
Robert McDougall Art Gallery,
Christchurch, New Zealand
Manawatu Museum,
Palmerston North, New Zealand
Dale Chihuly: Pelléas and Mélisande
Renwick Gallery, National Museum of American
Art, Smithsonian Institution,
Washington, D.C.

1995
Chihuly: alla Macchia
Polk Museum of Art,
Lakeland, Florida
Grace Museum,
Abilene, Texas
Chihuly Baskets
Washington State Historical Society Museum,
Tacoma, Washington
Maryhill Museum of Art,
Goldendale, Washington
Sheehan Gallery, Whitman College,
Walla Walla, Washington
Chihuly: Form from Fire
Saint John's Museum of Art,
Wilmington, North Carolina
*Chihuly in New Zealand: Glass and Works
on Paper*
Hawke's Bay Exhibition Centre,
Hastings, New Zealand
Auckland Museum,
Auckland, New Zealand
Dale Chihuly
Jundt Art Museum, Gonzaga University,
Spokane, Washington
Dale Chihuly: Installations
Anchorage Museum of History and Art,
Anchorage, Alaska
San Jose Museum of Art,
San Jose, California
Dale Chihuly: On Site
Jacksonville Museum of Contemporary Art,
Jacksonville, Florida

1996
Alaska Baskets
Alutiiq Museum and Archaeological Repository,
Kodiak, Alaska
Sheldon Museum and Cultural Center,
Haines, Alaska
Sheldon Jackson Museum,
Sitka, Alaska
Chihuly: alla Macchia
Brevard Museum of Art and Science,
Melbourne, Florida
Leigh Yawkey Woodson Art Museum,
Wausau, Wisconsin
Chihuly Baskets
Art Museum of Missoula,

Missoula, Montana
Schneider Museum of Art,
Southern Oregon State College,
Ashland, Oregon
University of Wyoming Art Museum,
Laramie, Wyoming
Scottsdale Center for the Arts,
Scottsdale, Arizona
Chihuly Over Venice
Kemper Museum of Contemporary Art & Design,
Kansas City, Missouri
Chihuly: Seaforms
Corcoran Gallery of Art,
Washington, D.C.
Museum of Art, Williams College,
Williamstown, Massachusetts
Portland Museum of Art,
Portland, Maine
Crystal Gardens
LongHouse Foundation,
East Hampton, New York
Dale Chihuly: Installations
Contemporary Arts Center,
New Orleans, Louisiana
Baltimore Museum of Art,
Baltimore, Maryland
Saint Louis Art Museum,
St. Louis, Missouri
Dale Chihuly: On Site
Palm Springs Desert Museum,
Palm Springs, California

1997
Alaska Baskets
Carrie M. McLain Memorial Museum,
Nome, Alaska
Pratt Museum,
Homer, Alaska
Valdez Museum and Historical Archive,
Valdez, Alaska
Tongass Historical Museum,
Ketchikan, Alaska
Chihuly Baskets
Allied Arts Association,
Richland, Washington
Prichard Art Gallery, University of Idaho,
Moscow, Idaho
Chihuly: The George R. Stroemple Collection
Portland Art Museum,
Portland, Oregon
Chihuly Over Venice
Corcoran Gallery of Art,
Washington, D.C.
Portland Art Museum,
Portland, Oregon
Chihuly: Seaforms
Middlebury College Museum of Art,
Middlebury, Vermont
Everson Museum of Art,
Syracuse, New York

Heckscher Museum of Art,
Huntington, New York
Dale Chihuly: Installations
Minneapolis Institute of Arts,
Minneapolis, Minnesota
Dixon Gallery and Gardens,
Memphis, Tennessee
Albright-Knox Art Gallery,
Buffalo, New York
The Magic of Chihuly Glass
Kobe City Museum,
Kobe, Japan
Suntory Museum of Art,
Tokyo, Japan

1998
Alaska Baskets
Skagway Museum and Archives,
Skagway, Alaska
Chihuly Baskets
West Sound Arts Council,
Bremerton, Washington
Alaska State Museum,
Juneau, Alaska
Chihuly Over Venice
Columbus Museum of Art,
Columbus, Ohio
Chihuly: Seaforms
Memorial Art Gallery, University of Rochester,
Rochester, New York
New Britain Museum of American Art,
New Britain, Connecticut
Ball State University Museum of Art,
Muncie, Indiana
Dale Chihuly: Installations
Norton Museum of Art,
West Palm Beach, Florida
Dale Chihuly: On Site
Albuquerque Museum of Art and History,
Albuquerque, New Mexico
The Magic of Chihuly Glass
Fukuoka Art Museum,
Fukuoka, Japan
Montana Macchia
Holter Museum of Art,
Helena, Montana
Paris Gibson Square Museum of Art,
Great Falls, Montana
Hockaday Center for the Arts,
Kalispell, Montana
Custer County Art Center,
Miles City, Montana
Dale Chihuly
University Art Gallery, University of
California–San Diego,
La Jolla, California
Chihuly: The George R. Stroemple Collection
Akron Art Museum,
Akron, Ohio

Dale Chihuly: Venetians
Providence Athenaeum,
Providence, Rhode Island

1999
Chihuly in the Light of Jerusalem 2000
Tower of David Museum of the
History of Jerusalem,
Jerusalem, Israel
Chihuly Baskets
Delaware Art Museum,
Wilmington, Delaware
Plains Art Museum,
Fargo, North Dakota
Chihuly Over Venice
Columbus Museum of Art,
Columbus, Ohio
Chihuly: Glass Master
Hsinchu Municipal Cultural Center,
Hsinchu, Taiwan
Chihuly: Macchia
Northwest Art Center, Minot State University,
Minot, North Dakota
North Dakota Museum of Art,
Grand Forks, North Dakota
Rourke Art Gallery,
Moorhead, Minnesota
Chihuly: Seaforms
Palmer Museum of Art, Pennsylvania
State University,
University Park, Pennsylvania
Indianapolis Museum of Art, Columbus Gallery,
Columbus, Indiana
Dale Chihuly: Installations
Hiroshima City Museum of Contemporary Art,
Hiroshima, Japan
Contemporary Art Center of Virginia,
Virginia Beach, Virginia
Mint Museum of Craft + Design,
Charlotte, North Carolina
Dale Chihuly: Masterworks in Glass
National Gallery of Australia,
Canberra, Australia
*Dale Chihuly: The George R.
Stroemple Collection*
California Center for the Arts,
Escondido, California

2000
Chihuly Baskets
Braithwaite Fine Arts Gallery, Southern
Utah University,
Cedar City, Utah
Brigham Young University Museum of Art,
Provo, Utah
Chihuly: Inside and Out
Joslyn Art Museum,
Omaha, Nebraska

Chihuly: Seaforms
Fuller Museum of Art,
Brockton, Massachusetts
Fayetteville Museum of Art,
Fayetteville, North Carolina
Dale Chihuly: Installations
Knoxville Museum of Art,
Knoxville, Tennessee
Arkansas Arts Center,
Little Rock, Arkansas
Chihuly in Iceland: Form from Fire
Listasafn Reykjavíkur,
Reykjavík, Iceland
*Reflections of Chihuly: A Naples Museum
of Art Inaugural Exhibition*
Naples Museum of Art,
Naples, Florida
Dale Chihuly: On Site
Nevada Museum of Art,
Reno, Nevada
*Dale Chihuly: The George R.
Stroemple* Collection
San Jose Museum of Art,
San Jose, California
Chihuly: Masterworks in Glass
JamFactory Contemporary Craft and Design,
Adelaide, Australia

2001
Chihuly Seaforms
Bowers Museum of Cultural Art,
Santa Ana, California
Springfield Museum of Fine Arts,
Springfield, Massachusetts
Southern Vermont Art Center,
Manchester, Vermont
Chihuly Baskets
Crocker Art Museum,
Sacramento, California
Loveland Museum of Art,
Loveland, Colorado
Lauren Rogers Museum of Art,
Laurel, Mississippi
Tyler Museum of Art,
Tyler, Texas
Chihuly at the V&A
Victoria and Albert Museum,
London, England
Form from Fire: Glass Works by Dale Chihuly
Dayton Art Institute,
Dayton, Ohio
*Dale Chihuly: The George R.
Stroemple* Collection
Las Vegas Art Museum,
Las Vegas, Nevada
Boise Art Museum,
Boise, Idaho
Chihuly Over Venice
Milwaukee Art Museum,
Milwaukee, Wisconsin

MUSEUM COLLECTIONS

Akita Senshu Museum of Art, Akita, Japan
Akron Art Museum, Akron, Ohio
Albany Museum of Art, Albany, Georgia
Albright-Knox Art Gallery, Buffalo, New York
Allied Arts Association, Richland, Washington
American Craft Museum, New York, New York
Amon Carter Museum, Fort Worth, Texas
Anchorage Museum of History and Art, Anchorage, Alaska
Arizona State University Art Museum, Tempe, Arizona
Arkansas Arts Center, Little Rock, Arkansas
Art Gallery of Greater Victoria, Victoria, British Columbia, Canada
Art Gallery of Western Australia, Perth, Australia
Art Museum of Missoula, Missoula, Montana
Art Museum of Southeast Texas, Beaumont, Texas
Asheville Art Museum, Asheville, North Carolina
Auckland Museum, Auckland, New Zealand
Azabu Museum of Arts and Crafts, Tokyo, Japan
Ball State University Museum of Art, Muncie, Indiana
Beach Museum of Art, Kansas State University, Manhattan, Kansas
Bellevue Art Museum, Bellevue, Washington
Berkeley Art Museum, University of California, Berkeley, California
Birmingham Museum of Art, Birmingham, Alabama
Boarman Arts Center, Martinsburg, West Virginia
Boca Raton Museum of Art, Boca Raton, Florida
Brooklyn Museum, Brooklyn, New York
Canadian Craft Museum, Vancouver, British Columbia, Canada
Carnegie Museum of Art, Pittsburgh, Pennsylvania
Charles A. Wustum Museum of Fine Arts, Racine, Wisconsin
Chrysler Museum of Art, Norfolk, Virginia
Cincinnati Art Museum, Cincinnati, Ohio
Cleveland Center for Contemporary Art, Cleveland, Ohio
Cleveland Museum of Art, Cleveland, Ohio
Columbus Cultural Arts Center, Columbus, Ohio
Columbus Museum of Art, Columbus, Ohio
Contemporary Arts Center, Cincinnati, Ohio
Contemporary Museum, Honolulu, Hawaii
Cooper-Hewitt, National Design Museum, Smithsonian Institution, New York, New York
Corning Museum of Glass, Corning, New York
Crocker Art Museum, Sacramento, California
Currier Gallery of Art, Manchester, New Hampshire
Daiichi Museum, Nagoya, Japan
Dallas Museum of Art, Dallas, Texas
Danske Kunstindustrimuseum, Copenhagen, Denmark
Dayton Art Institute, Dayton, Ohio
DeCordova Museum and Sculpture Park, Lincoln, Massachusetts
Delaware Art Museum, Wilmington, Delaware
Denver Art Museum, Denver, Colorado
Detroit Institute of Arts, Detroit, Michigan
Dowse Art Museum, Lower Hutt, New Zealand
Elvehjem Museum of Art, University of Wisconsin, Madison, Wisconsin
Eretz Israel Museum, Tel Aviv, Israel
Everson Museum of Art, Syracuse, New York
Fine Arts Institute, Edmond, Oklahoma
Flint Institute of Arts, Flint, Michigan
Glasmuseum, Ebeltoft, Denmark
Glasmuseum, Frauenau, Germany
Glasmuseum alter Hof Herding, Glascollection, Ernsting, Germany
Glasmuseum Wertheim, Wertheim, Germany
Grand Rapids Art Museum, Grand Rapids, Michigan
Hakone Glass Forest, Ukai Museum, Hakone, Japan
Hawke's Bay Exhibition Centre, Hastings, New Zealand
High Museum of Art, Atlanta, Georgia

Hiroshima City Museum of Contemporary Art, Hiroshima, Japan
Hokkaido Museum of Modern Art, Hokkaido, Japan
Honolulu Academy of Arts, Honolulu, Hawaii
Hunter Museum of American Art, Chattanooga, Tennessee
Indianapolis Museum of Art, Indianapolis, Indiana
Israel Museum, Jerusalem, Israel
Japan Institute of Arts and Crafts, Tokyo, Japan
Jesse Besser Museum, Alpena, Michigan
Joslyn Art Museum, Omaha, Nebraska
Jundt Art Museum, Gonzaga University, Spokane, Washington
Kalamazoo Institute of Arts, Kalamazoo, Michigan
Kaohsiung Museum of Fine Arts, Kaohsiung, Taiwan
Kemper Museum of Contemporary Art & Design, Kansas City, Missouri
Kestner-Gesellschaft, Hannover, Germany
Kobe City Museum, Kobe, Japan
Krannert Art Museum, University of Illinois, Champaign, Illinois
Krasl Art Center, St. Joseph, Michigan
Kunstmuseum Düsseldorf, Düsseldorf, Germany
Kunstsammlungen der Veste Coburg, Coburg, Germany
Kurita Museum, Tochigi, Japan
Leigh Yawkey Woodson Art Museum, Wausau, Wisconsin
Lobmeyr Museum, Vienna, Austria
Los Angeles County Museum of Art, Los Angeles, California
Lowe Art Museum, University of Miami, Coral Gables, Florida
Lyman Allyn Art Museum, New London, Connecticut
M.H. de Young Memorial Museum, San Francisco, California
Madison Art Center, Madison, Wisconsin
Manawatu Museum, Palmerston North, New Zealand
Matsushita Art Museum, Kagoshima, Japan
Meguro Museum of Art, Tokyo, Japan
Memorial Art Gallery, University of Rochester, Rochester, New York
Metropolitan Museum of Art, New York, New York
Milwaukee Art Museum, Milwaukee, Wisconsin
Minneapolis Institute of Arts, Minneapolis, Minnesota
Mint Museum of Craft + Design, Charlotte, North Carolina
Mobile Museum of Art, Mobile, Alabama
Modern Art Museum of Fort Worth, Fort Worth, Texas
Morris Museum, Morristown, New Jersey
Musée d'Art Moderne et d'Art Contemporain, Nice, France
Musée des Arts Décoratifs, Lausanne, Switzerland
Musée des Arts Décoratifs, Palais du Louvre, Paris, France
Musée des Arts Décoratifs de Montréal, Montreal, Quebec, Canada
Musée des Beaux-Arts et de la Céramique, Rouen, France
Musée Provincial Sterckshof, Antwerp, Belgium
Museo del Vidrio, Monterrey, Mexico
Museum Bellerive, Zurich, Switzerland
Museum Boijmans Van Beuningen, Rotterdam, The Netherlands
Museum für Kunst und Gewerbe Hamburg, Hamburg, Germany
Museum für Kunsthandwerk, Frankfurt am Main, Germany
Museum of American Glass at Wheaton Village, Millville, New Jersey
Museum of Art, Fort Lauderdale, Florida
Museum of Art, Rhode Island School of Design, Providence, Rhode Island
Museum of Art and Archaeology, Columbia, Missouri
Museum of Arts and Sciences, Daytona Beach, Florida
Museum of Contemporary Art, Chicago, Illinois
Museum of Contemporary Art at San Diego, La Jolla, California
Museum of Fine Arts, Boston, Massachusetts
Museum of Fine Arts, St. Petersburg, Florida
Museum of Modern Art, New York, New York
Museum of Northwest Art, La Conner, Washington
Museum voor Sierkunst en Vormgeving, Ghent, Belgium
Muskegon Museum of Art, Muskegon, Michigan

Muzeum města Brna, Brno, Czech Republic
Muzeum skla a bižuterie, Jablonec nad Nisou, Czech Republic
Naples Museum of Art, Naples, Florida
National Gallery of Australia, Canberra, Australia
National Gallery of Victoria, Melbourne, Australia
National Liberty Museum, Philadelphia, Pennsylvania
National Museum Kyoto, Kyoto, Japan
National Museum of American History, Smithsonian Institution, Washington, D.C.
National Museum of Modern Art Kyoto, Kyoto, Japan
National Museum of Modern Art Tokyo, Tokyo, Japan
Nationalmuseum, Stockholm, Sweden
New Orleans Museum of Art, New Orleans, Louisiana
Niijima Contemporary Art Museum, Niijima, Japan
North Central Washington Museum, Wenatchee, Washington
Notojima Glass Art Museum, Ishikawa, Japan
O Art Museum, Tokyo, Japan
Otago Museum, Dunedin, New Zealand
Palm Springs Desert Museum, Palm Springs, California
Palmer Museum of Art, Pennsylvania State University, University Park, Pennsylvania
Parrish Art Museum, Southampton, New York
Philadelphia Museum of Art, Philadelphia, Pennsylvania
Phoenix Art Museum, Phoenix, Arizona
Plains Art Museum, Fargo, North Dakota
Portland Art Museum, Portland, Oregon
Powerhouse Museum, Sydney, Australia
Princeton University Art Museum, Princeton, New Jersey
Queensland Art Gallery, South Brisbane, Australia
Robert McDougall Art Gallery, Christchurch, New Zealand
Royal Ontario Museum, Toronto, Ontario, Canada
Saint Louis Art Museum, St. Louis, Missouri
Samuel P. Harn Museum of Art, University of Florida, Gainesville, Florida
San Francisco Museum of Modern Art, San Francisco, California
San Jose Museum of Art, San Jose, California
Scitech Discovery Centre, Perth, Australia
Scottsdale Center for the Arts, Scottsdale, Arizona
Seattle Art Museum, Seattle, Washington
Shimonoseki City Art Museum, Shimonoseki, Japan
Singapore Art Museum, Singapore
Smith College Museum of Art, Northampton, Massachusetts
Smithsonian American Art Museum, Washington, D.C.
Sogetsu Art Museum, Tokyo, Japan
Speed Art Museum, Louisville, Kentucky
Spencer Museum of Art, University of Kansas, Lawrence, Kansas
Springfield Museum of Fine Arts, Springfield, Massachusetts
Suntory Museum of Art, Tokyo, Japan
Suomen Lasimuseo, Riihimäki, Finland
Suwa Garasu no Sato Museum, Nagano, Japan
Tacoma Art Museum, Tacoma, Washington
Taipei Fine Arts Museum, Taipei, Taiwan
Tochigi Prefectural Museum of Fine Arts, Tochigi, Japan
Toledo Museum of Art, Toledo, Ohio
Uměleckoprůmyslové muzeum, Prague, Czech Republic
Utah Museum of Fine Arts, University of Utah, Salt Lake City, Utah
Victoria and Albert Museum, London, England
Wadsworth Atheneum, Hartford, Connecticut
Waikato Museum of Art and History, Hamilton, New Zealand
Whatcom Museum of History and Art, Bellingham, Washington
White House Collection of American Crafts, Washington, D.C.
Whitney Museum of American Art, New York, New York
Württembergisches Landesmuseum Stuttgart, Stuttgart, Germany
Yale University Art Gallery, New Haven, Connecticut
Yokohama Museum of Art, Yokohama, Japan

Published by V&A Publications in association
with Portland Press 2001

Photographs
Philip Amdal, Parks Anderson, Theresa Batty,
Dick Busher, Rachel Coates, Jody Coleman,
Jan Cook, Richard Davis, Claire Garoutte,
Sarah Hodges, Ken Jackson, Russell Johnson,
Scott M. Leen, Tom Lind, Teresa N. Rishel,
Terry Rishel, James Stevenson, and Chuck Taylor

Design Team
Anna Katherine Curfman, Laurence Madrelle,
Marie Pellaton, and Barry Rosen

Paper
Lumisilk matt art 150 gsm

Typefaces
Avenir and Grotesk No. 9

ISBN 1 85177 363 0

V&A Publications
160 Brompton Road
London SW3 1HW
www.vam.ac.uk

Printing and binding
C&C Offset Printing Co, Ltd. in Hong Kong

To Laurence Madrelle for 32 years
of great friendship